For Jane

With appreciation
and very best wishes

from staff and residents at
the Oxford Beaumont

January 1993

BERKSHIRE

of one hundred years ago

HINTON WALDRIST

THE STREET, ALDERMASTON

BERKSHIRE

of one hundred years ago

D A V I D   B U X T O N

BERKSHIRE BOOKS

First published in the United Kingdom in 1992 by Berkshire Books

British Library Cataloguing in Publication Data

A Catalogue record for this book is available from the British Library

ISBN 0-7509-0217-5

BERKSHIRE BOOKS
Official Imprint of Berkshire County Council
Managed by
Alan Sutton Publishing Ltd
Phoenix Mill · Far Thrupp · Stroud
Gloucestershire

READING

Typeset in 11/13 Bembo
Typesetting and origination by
Alan Sutton Publishing Limited.
Printed in Great Britain by
M. & A. Thomson Litho Ltd., East Kilbride, Scotland.

Preface

It has been my aim in *Berkshire of one hundred years ago* to try to recreate on the page some of the feel and flavour of the late nineteenth- and early twentieth-centuries in Berkshire. Old photographs give us the visual images of the period, the town streets, the lanes and village greens of the countryside but most interesting of all, the people. How our ancestors dressed, worked and played is of great interest to us and herein, probably, lies much of our nostalgic interest in old photographs. Costumes, hairstyles, moustaches and hats are the subject of much interest, if not amazement, to us, so different are they to late twentieth-century concepts of convenience and style. But in this book I have attempted to add to the interest of the photographs by placing alongside them extracts from contemporary writing on Berkshire. The text of the book is made up of short pieces taken from diaries and reminiscences, biographies, short stories and newscuttings, all written in or about Berkshire at the time of the photographs. We are fortunate that there is a wealth of such material available and that it covers such a wide range of places and people. Examples of some of the extremes I have used range from a village rector's warmly remembered accounts of rustic parishioners in East Lockinge of the 1890s to letters from Queen Victoria's Court written by one of her companions at Windsor. Whenever possible I have tried to match the text to appropriate photographs so that a story from a named village sits next to a contemporary picture of the same village. Sometimes the appropriateness of the matching is a little more fanciful.

Most of the photographs and texts chosen for the book date from the 1880s to just after the turn of the century and although some stray a few years outside these limits I have included them if I thought they made a useful contribution and were still typical of the late nineteenth-century period.

READING

1

DIDCOT

Although I have not attempted to include every town and village in the county the spread is geographically wide and I hope that most areas are fairly represented. It is important to remember, here, that Berkshire of the 1890s was encircled by different boundaries to the present county. This book includes all of the historic county of Berkshire, the northern part of which in 1974 became administratively part of modern Oxfordshire. Thus Abingdon, Faringdon, Wallingford, Wantage and Didcot and many of the villages of north Berkshire and the Downs are returned here to their historic home and are included in the book.

I have added only short captions to the photographs, usually sufficient to simply locate the scene, but fuller details, when available, are listed along with dates and sources at the end of the book. Text sources are also listed to give the opportunity of following up a book and reading it in the original.

Assembling the material for this book has given me much pleasure and I hope that the result will give as much pleasure to others. In producing it I have received help and advice from many people who have loaned photographs and books and given me useful research leads. A full list of photographic sources and acknowledgements is included at the end of the book but I should like to thank especially:

Michael Bott, Archivist, University of Reading; Alfred Brown, Morland's Brewery, Abingdon; Frances Dimond, Windsor Castle Royal Archives; Malcolm Graham, Centre for Oxfordshire Studies, Oxford; Tony Higgot, Newbury District Museum; Barbara Holden and Sadie Ward, Institute of Agricultural History and Museum of English Rural Life, University of Reading; Judith Hunter, Windsor Royal Borough Collection; Mr St. John Parker, Headmaster, Abingdon School; Dr. H. Pihlens, Hungerford; Sue Read, Blake's Lock Museum, Reading and Margaret Smith, Local Studies Library, Reading.

Last but not least I want to thank my own family Sue, Tom and Rupert for their help and patience whilst I was compiling this book.

David Buxton
September 1992

Introduction

Berkshire of a century ago, like most English counties, still saw most of its population employed on the land or in activities associated with agriculture and rural crafts. Although migration to the towns for those seeking work or an escape from low wages had been a tradition since the beginning of the Industrial Revolution, the latter part of the nineteenth century saw a further worsening of the plight of workers on the farms. A combination of events had brought this about. The repeal, in the mid-1800s, of the Corn Laws which had previously protected the English farmers from cheap grain imports from North America, had had an increasingly devastating effect on the home wheat market. Coupled with the falling prices many farming counties of the south of England had also suffered poor harvests caused by the succession of cold, wet summers of the late 1870s and early 1880s, resulting in the further loss of jobs on the farms and to the eventual bankruptcy of many farmers. Those that survived this period were often the ones who had adopted new methods and invested in new machinery; steam engines were beginning to take over from man- and horse-power. Mechanization of ploughing, harvesting and threshing led to greater efficiency but also another round of job losses for the labourers. By today's standards, though, farmwork was still labour intensive and amongst the pictures featured in this book, there are numerous examples of people harvesting and haymaking by hand. Some of these might be misleading; hence, the picture of a man using a hand flail to thresh wheat (p. 13) is most likely a record photograph taken to show a technique that was dying out whilst there was still someone to demonstrate it. Photographs of steam-driven threshing machines are much more common for this period.

Much of central and north Berkshire was home to large flocks of sheep, the county having been, since the Middle Ages, one of the foremost wool producing areas of the country. In the 1890s it would not have been possible to look at any part of the downs and not see sheep. Books about nineteenth-century Berkshire abound with descriptions and tales of sheep and shepherds, so much a part of the scene were they. The shepherd, although traditionally much revered for his patience and loyalty to his sheep was also an occasional figure of fun to his contemporaries because of his unworldliness and lack of learning. Whilst there may well have been some justification for this in some cases, there are none-the-less counter tales that credit other shepherds with a sharp wit and good humour. Shepherds were often good naturalists and forecasters of the weather.

Some of the largest sheep fairs in the country were held in Berkshire; the August fair at East Ilsley, for example, attracted up to eighty thousand sheep to the one-day event. This tiny, peaceful village would be swamped by the sheep penned in the streets, dogs barking and running, farmers and shepherds packing the inns and verges, a funfair and travelling traders of every description made the best of the gathering while they could. One can readily imagine the excitement of these occasions when one reads the first hand account written by a visitor who saw one around the turn of the century (pp. 76–80).

Although great changes were taking place in rural counties a century ago and there was a good deal of hardship, such things are not usually evident from the photographs we see of the period. Photographs were, of course, frequently posed views, just as they are now, and tended to show peaceful, idyllic scenes suggesting rural contentment. We should remember though that those romantic looking cottages were cold and damp and that their inhabitants were poor and could rarely afford good food or domestic comforts, a far cry from the modernized cottages of today in which it is possible to be comfortable and pretend to be living a rural lifestyle.

Working farm labourers would supplement the food they could buy with home-grown produce and perhaps a pig would be kept, fattened up on scraps, for the table. Not everyone could afford even this luxury and gardens in towns would have been rare. Newspapers of the time frequently reported sad cases of petty theft seen by the magistrate's courts in which food was often the item stolen. It says much about late Victorian values that someone who stole a cabbage from a garden or poached a rabbit from the estate of a rich man could receive a punitive sentence for this desperate attempt to feed his family. This unsympathetic attitude to poverty is exempli-

CROWN INN, HURST

fied nowhere more typically than in that most infamous example of Victorian institutions, the union workhouse. Ostensibly set up to provide relief and accommodation for those that through ill-health or old age could no longer support themselves, they were deliberately made unappealing and harsh so as not to attract the malingerer. The union workhouses replaced parish relief and poor houses in 1834 and were administered by a Board of Guardians. The workhouses were loathed and feared by the poor and understandably so. Whilst there seems to have been considerable variation between 'unions' in the type of care offered, many had notorious reputations for cruel and unsympathetic regimes. Many workhouses continued to exist, run on the same principles, well into this century, with somewhat improved conditions, but with little improvement in reputation. A letter to the *Reading Observer* in 1892 seeking to improve the poor public image of the Reading Union Workhouse (see p. 21) tells us instead more about the entrenched views of the establishment at the time. The writer of the letter was a middle-class man who, writing from his position of domestic security, felt able to talk cheerfully, but patronizingly, about the attributes of this grim establishment. One is left wondering how he himself would have coped if faced with the prospect of an enforced retirement within its walls.

Whilst there were unpleasant aspects to life in Victorian England for the less well off it has to be said that life was not all hardship and pain. There are examples among the pieces here that describe the lighter side of life. Pleasures were often simpler ones by our late twentieth-century standards; story-telling round the fire or in the inn, harvest-homes (with beer and food at the farmer's expense), pranks played on unfortunate neighbours and the making (and drinking) of country wines. Life had cycles of events that we notice less today, those dictated by the seasons of the farming year and the church. Thus harvest, haymaking, fruit-picking, sheep and horse fairs, agricultural shows, Christmas and Easter all brought with them a holiday or a diversion from the otherwise dull routine.

We have looked at life mainly in the countryside so far, and this is appropriate since that is where most people lived and worked at this time and is also the part most represented in this book, but we must not ignore the towns. The largest of these and the place with the most industry was, as it is now, the town of Reading. Here was a relative hive of industrial development, with many people employed in its factories, shops and service occupations. The largest of the factories was certainly that of Huntley and Palmers in Kings Road. The company had begun biscuit production in the first quarter of the century but by the 1850s had begun to introduce methods of mass production that were probably the first of their kind in the world. By the 1890s the firm was employing about four thousand people and exporting biscuits all over the world.

Reading could also boast of the biggest brewery in the county, Simonds in Bridge Street, which was not only an early wholesaler of beer but also ran local banking. Another national name that was famous in Reading at the time was that of Sutton's Seeds. So busy was the town at this time developing its business and building houses for its workers that perhaps it failed to look after its appearances; it certainly did not impress one traveller, James Vincent, who having passed through at the turn of the century wrote in his *Highways and Byways of Berkshire*:

Neither, just now, will we halt to look at Caversham, unlovely suburb of Reading, nor linger in Reading itself.

HENRY WILDER'S STUDIO, SULHAM

For Reading, rich in memories and in history, is poor in relics and in beauty. Most of it looks as bare and newly baked as one of the biscuits of Reading fame, and the one tolerable thing seen as you pass in the train is found in the flashing bands and beds of colour from Messrs Sutton's nursery grounds. Nothing or next to nothing is gained by entering the town. Some of the churches possess features of interest in detail. But on the whole the town that was taken by the Danes in 871 ... is as plain and prosperous a conglomeration of dull houses, and one seeming to breathe the air of history as little, as any that is to be found in England.

Of the smaller towns, most appear as the quiet market towns that they probably were, untroubled by the traffic and bustle of today, whilst communities on the river Thames like Maidenhead, Cookham and Pangbourne are so often portrayed in photographs as centres for holidays on the water that we could be forgiven for imagining that this was how they looked all of the time. In the Royal town of Windsor the frequent comings and goings of the world's royalty to the castle and the court of Queen Victoria were a familiar sight to the residents of the town, scenes of richness that were apparently somewhat at odds with the experience of those living outside the walls of that famous castle. Contemporary accounts of the town of Windsor report that some of the worst poverty and slum conditions in the county existed on the Queen's doorstep.

Of the Berkshire writers from whom I have borrowed material for this collection few are well-known names or national characters but there were those who had special knowledge or memories of a particular village or area that can give a glimpse of a time now past. Eleanor Hayden, the daughter of the Revd Frederick Hayden, rector of West Hendred, wrote several books about her village. Her attractive style made use of dialect speech for her characters and her work was popular around the turn of the century, although James Vincent was patronizing when he reviewed her books at the time:

The books have humour too, although their world is necessarily narow and they are perforce somewhat over-weighted by dialect. Above all they are true. But let me not make the mistake of rating Miss Hayden's work too high. She has not the relentless strength of Thomas Hardy ... certainly those who desire to know the ways of the Berkshire peasantry, their old world customs, their hard life ... cannot do better than face the struggle against their dialect in Miss Hayden's books...

I think him too hard on her, try this sample of her writing in which she describes children trying to catch a crayfish:

Ther' usted to be two on 'um, a li'le crawfish an' a girt 'un as bid in a hole anighst the bridge. We tried a smart few times to catch 'un, but 'un war too cunnin' an' 'udn't quilt the worm. One on us tried to scroop 'un up in his hat, but they 'udn't be scrope, so we fot a close-prop an'

FRANCES DANN, PHOTOGRAPHER

hucked out the girt 'un – the li'le un he flod away under the arch, wher 'un ha'nt sin 'un sence.

It is notable that we often rely for accounts of rural life in earlier times upon the writings of the village clergy. This is perhaps not surprising, since they were amongst the handful of educated people in the village, their calling brought them into contact with all and sundry and they had the leisure time in which to write. One thinks of Kilvert, Woodforde amd Witts in other counties but in Berkshire James Cornish, Rector of East Lockinge and later Vicar of Sunningdale and Peter Ditchfield, Rector of Barkham are local examples in this tradition. Both left sympathetic accounts of life in their villages around the turn of the century and I have used some pieces from their writings in this book.

We should be grateful too for the likes of Emma Thoyts, a Berkshire lady with a passion for collecting children's games and rhymes. She toured the county in the latter years of the last century noting down what she heard and saw in school playground and on village green to make the most comprehensive record of children's play available on the county. She wrote it all down in beautiful, copperplate long-hand and one can still read it in its original form in a local library. I have transcribed some and included them in the book.

Now what of the Berkshire photographers? The father of modern photography William Henry Fox Talbot chose Berkshire in which to establish the world's first commercial photographic establishment. Following his early experiments with the photographic process at his home in Lacock, Wiltshire in 1834, he announced and patented his technique, the first to use a negative, in 1839. In 1843, with his assistant and friend Nicholas Hennemen, he established his commercial premises in an old school building at Russell Terrace, Reading. They were initially secretive about their plans. Suspicions about Hennemen's behaviour were aroused and are recalled by John Henderson who later became an assistant at the establishment:

> Reading was a comparatively small town at that time, and any new resident was sure to cause some attention, especially if a foreigner; constant visits to our shop where he purchased every kind of writing paper we could supply, and then going direct to a well known chemist for various chemicals not in general use, soon aroused suspicion as to his vocation; he lived alone with an old house-keeper in a tolerably good house which had been a school, where there was a large room without windows … always kept locked; prying neighbours and others who made enquiries about him soon came to the conclusion that he was engaged in forging foreign bank notes or some nefarious pursuit.

Once set up, the establishment produced prints from Fox Talbot's negatives for commercial sale in bookshops and stationers and they offered to photograph customer's valuable effects, such as paintings and statues, their houses or themselves. They also offered to teach the technique to others but only under a special licence for amateur use. The business appears not to have been a great commercial success and after about four years Hennemen moved the enterprise to London. A series of

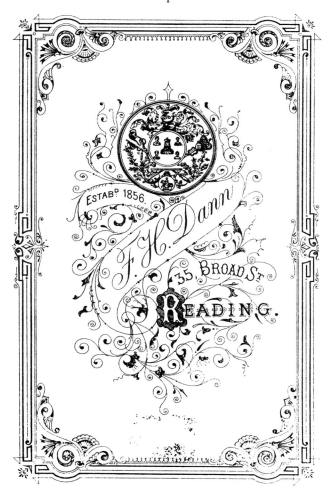

photographs of Reading in the 1840s are an important legacy of this period but are too early for inclusion in this book!

Forty to fifty years on, Berkshire was rich in commercial photographic studios. The technique of photography, though still improving, was more reliable and photography was a popular hobby, at least with the better off. Of this period the name of one practitioner is prominent in the north Berkshire area and along the valley of the Thames, and that is of the Oxford-based photographer Henry Taunt. Born at about the time that Fox Talbot was setting up in Reading, he was apprenticed to a photographer at the age of fourteen and set up on his own in Oxford in 1868. He is thought to have taken around 53,000 photographs in his career and is best known for his pictures of the Thames and its surrounding villages. He was a skilled technician with the camera but also had a very good eye for a picture. Some examples of his best photographs illustrate this book.

Of the many other late Victorian and Edwardian photographers of Berkshire I have drawn on three or four in particular, chosen because of the quality of their pictures and because many of their original negatives have been preserved. Whenever possible these have been used for the prints used in this book. These include photographs by Llewellyn Treacher who worked from Twyford, Phillip Osborne Collier who had studios in Waylen Street and later in Oxford Street, Reading, and Frances Dann, Berkshire's first professional woman photographer. Frances Dann set up her first studio in 1856 in Broad Street, Reading and after her marriage to Henry Lewis, a presenter of Magic Lantern shows, renamed the business 'Dann Lewis' although Henry never took any part in the photography. Her skill as a photographer and business woman ensured that the firm continued well into this century and was eventually taken over by her granddaughter, also Frances, who ran it until the beginning of the Second World War. It is rarer to find good collections of the work of private photographers of this period, presumably because these were not as common as the commercial ones, but we are fortunate that some of the photographs and the albums of Henry Beaufoy Wilder of Sulham House have survived. He was a keen and skilled amateur with his own well-equipped studio at Sulham and a specially built carriage to carry his equipment on excursions.

Now, having looked briefly at the historical background to the setting of the book and introduced some of the many writers and photographers whose work forms the source material, I hope that you will now go on to enjoy this new and modern presentation of their work. The book follows in a long tradition — the very first photographically illustrated book, *The Pencil of Nature* by Fox Talbot, was prepared for publication in Reading at the author's premises in Russell Terrace in 1844 and received the following review:

> The experiment of photographically illustrated books is now before the world; and all who see Mr Talbot's publication will be convinced that the promise of the art of it is great and its utility and excellence, in many respects, of a high order.

The Athenaeum, February 22 1845

BERKSHIRE

of one hundred years ago

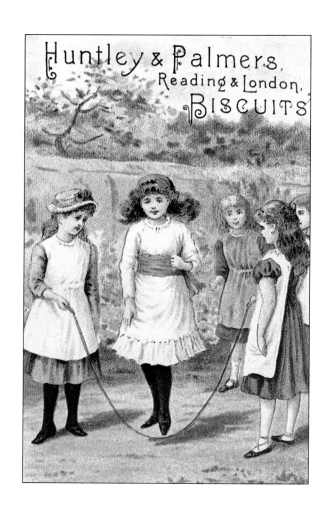

BERKSHIRE DOWNS NEAR WEST ILSLEY

TOM BROWN'S HOLIDAYS

Now in my time, when we got home by the old coach, which puts us down at the cross-roads with our boxes the first day of the holidays, and had been driven off by the family coachman, singing 'Dulce domum' at the top of our voices, there we were, fixtures, till Black Monday came round. We had to cut out our own amusements within a walk or a ride of home. And so we got to know all the country folk, and their ways and songs and stories, by heart; and went over the fields and wolds and hills, again and again, till we made friends of them all. We were Berkshire, or Gloucestershire, or Yorkshire boys, and you're young cosmopolites, belonging to all counties and no countries. No doubt it's all right, I dare say it is. This is the day of large views and glorious humanity, and all that; but I wish back-sword play hadn't gone out in the Vale of White Horse, and that that confounded Great Western hadn't carried away Alfred's Hill to make an embankment.

But to return to the said Vale of White Horse, the country in which the first scenes of this true and interesting story are laid. As I said, the Great Western now runs right through it, and it is a land of large rich pastures, bounded by ox-fences, and covered with fine hedgerow timber, with here and there a nice little gorse or spinney, where abideth poor Charley, having no other cover to which to betake himself for miles and miles, when pushed out some fine November morning by the Old Berkshire. Those who have been there, and well mounted, only know how he, and the stanch little pack who dash after him, heads high and sterns low, with a breast-high scent, can consume the ground at such times. There being little plough-land, and few woods, the Vale is only an average sporting country, except for hunting. The villages are straggling, queer, old-fashioned places, the houses being dropped down without the least regularity, in nooks and out-of-the-way corners, by the sides of shadowy lanes and footpaths, each with its patch of garden. They are built chiefly of good grey stone and thatched, though I see that within the last year or two the red-brick cottages are multiplying, for the Vale is beginning to manufacture largely both brick and tiles. There are lots of waste ground by the side of the roads in every village, amounting often to village greens, where feed the pigs and ganders of the people; and these roads are old-fashioned, homely roads, very dirty and badly made, and hardly endurable in winter, but still pleasant jog-trot roads, running through the great pasture lands, dotted here and there with little clumps of thorns, where the sleek kine [cows] are feeding, with no fence on either side of them, and a gate at the end of each field, which makes you get out of your gig (if you keep one), and gives you a chance of looking about you every quarter of a mile.

THE SCHOOLHOUSE, HINTON WALDRIST

One of the moralists whom we sat under in my youth – was it the great Richard Swiveller, or Mr Stiggins? – says, 'we are born in a vale, and must take the consequences of being found in such a situation.' These consequences, I for one am ready to encounter. I pity people who weren't born in a vale. I don't mean a flat country, but a vale; that is, a flat country bounded by hills. The having your hill *always* in view if you choose to turn towards him, that's the essence of a vale. There he is for ever, in the distance, your friend and companion; you never lose him as you do in hilly districts.

And then what a hill is the White Horse Hill! There it stands right up above all the rest, nine hundred feet above the sea, and the boldest, bravest shape for a chalk hill that you ever saw. Let us go up to the top of him, and see what is to be found there. Aye, you may well wonder, and think it odd you never heard of this before; but, wonder or not, as you please, there are hundreds of such things lying about England, which wiser folk than you know nothing of, and care nothing for. Yes, it's a magnificent Roman camp, and no mistake, with gates, and ditch, and mounds, all as complete as it was twenty years after the strong old rogues left it. Here, right up on the highest point, from which they say you can see eleven counties, they trenched round all the table-land, some twelve or fourteen acres, as was their custom, for they couldn't bear anybody to overlook them, and made their eyrie. The ground falls away rapidly on all sides. Was there ever such turf in the whole world? You sink up to your ankles at every step, and yet the spring of it is delicious. There is always a breeze in the 'camp', as it is called, and here it lies, just

as the Romans left it, except that cairn on the east side, left by her Majesty's choir of Sappers and Miners the other day, when they and the Engineer Officer had finished their sojourn there, and their surveys for the Ordnance Map of Berkshire. It is altogether a place that you won't forget – a place to open a man's soul and make him prophesy, as he looks down on that great Vale, spread out as the garden of the Lord before him, and wave on wave of the mysterious downs behind; and to the right and left the chalk hills running away into the distance, along which he can trace for miles the old Roman road, 'the Ridgeway' (the 'Rudge' as the country-folk call it), keeping straight along the highest back of the hills – such a place as Balak brought Balaam to, and told him to prophesy against the people in the valley beneath. And he could not, neither shall you, for they are a people of the Lord who abide there.

And now we leave the camp, and descend towards the west, and are on the Ash-down. We are treading on heroes. It is sacred ground for Englishmen, more sacred than all but one or two fields where their bones lie whitening. For this is the actual place where our Alfred won his great battle, the battle of Ash-down ('æscendun' in the chroniclers) which broke the Danish power, and made England a Christian land. The Danes held the camp, and the slope where we are standing, the whole crown of the hill in fact. 'The heathen had beforehand seized the higher ground,' as old Asser says, having wasted everything behind them from London, and being just ready to burst down on the fair vale, Alfred's own birthplace and heritage. And up the heights came the Saxons, as they did at the Alma. 'The Christians led up their

10

CHAPEL LANE, UFFINGTON

line from the lower ground. There stood also on that same spot a single thorn-tree, marvellous stumpy (which we ourselves with our very own eyes have seen).' Bless the old chronicler! does he think nobody ever saw the 'single thorn-tree' but himself? Why, there it stands to this very day, just on the edge of the slope, and I saw it not three weeks since; and old single thorn-tree, 'marvellous stumpy.' At least if it isn't the same tree, it ought to have been, for it's just in the place where the battle must have been won or lost – 'around which,' as I was saying, 'the two lines of foemen came together in battle with a huge shout. And in this place, one of the two Kings of the heathen and five of his earls fell down and died, and many thousands of the heathen side in the same place.' After which crowning mercy, the pious King, that there might never be wanting a sign and a memorial to the countryside, carved out on the northern side of the chalk hill, under the camp, where it is almost precipitous, the great Saxon white horse, which he who will may see from the railway, and which gives its name to the vale, over which it has looked these thousand years and more.

Thomas Hughes

DROUGHT

In 1893, the year that I lived at Faringdon, we endured a drought which was really terrible. From February 28th to May 16th no measurable rain fell, and by the end of April the grass,

even in the Thames-side meadows, was brown, and dandelions covered the meadows with their white seed heads. No rain had fallen to knock off the tufts of seed, and the grass was not tall enough to hide them. Old inhabitants said that there had not been so dry a spring since 1844, when the farmers cut boughs from the elm trees to feed their cattle, and when at length rain did fall the report in *The Times* showed that the local tradition was pretty accurate. In 1844 the drought lasted from March 11th to June 23rd. In 1893 we had a brief respite in May, but early in June the heat began again, and all through that summer the farmers were at their wits' end to find food for their animals. Hay cost £7 a ton, and there was little to be had even at that price. I saw cattle being fed in the meadows with unthreshed oats, and was told of one farmer who offered his flock of sheep to a neighbour for 5s. a piece, but the reply was in the negative. 'Well then, I will *give* them to you, I cannot bear to see the poor things suffer.' The answer was, 'No, thank you, I will not have one more thing that has a mouth on my farm.'

One never saw cows lying down and peacefully chewing the cud under the trees, they seemed to be always walking about looking for something to eat in the brown pastures. But where the grazing cattle had access to a supply of clean water they kept in fairly good condition. The grass was nutritious though short, and the sunshine favourable for health, so the bullocks did far better than the milch cows. But it was sad to see the condition of the cattle on the small holdings where the owners were too poor to buy feeding stuffs, and the meadows,

11

MILL STREET, WANTAGE

even in ordinary years, were of poor quality. Some of them used to pass the windows of my lodgings every day, and week by week they looked thinner and more wretched. Though the absolute drought ended on May 17th, yet June, July and August were very dry months and the temperatures extremely high. The corn on the light soil was thin and stunted, and the root-crops almost a complete failure. There may have been years since then with less rain, but I do not know of one which was harder on the cattle.

James Cornish

THRESHING

Sheening [threshing], though a thirsty employment, is not unpopular. It is a variation of the ordinary farm routine; it means increased pay always, extra beer sometimes; and besides the excitement of mice and rat hunts, it offers exceptional facilities for the interchange of gossip. Both sexes are represented, and as the workpeople are occupied within a small area, items of local interest, scraps of scandal, opinions on men and manners can be shouted across from the diminishing wheat rick to its rising straw companion, and up from the engine to the box, while the work goes merrily forward to the machine's droning song.

What a pleasant sound is that song! Heard on a still autumn day when the sunshine is sleeping on the hills, and the trees have doffed their green robes for russet garb or golden, it tunes its note to the pensive landscape and floats in melancholy cadence over the deserted fields – stripped to supply the burden of the music. In the sweet springtide, when the world is wakening to new life, it seems to hum more cheerily and to echo the promise given when time was young, that while the earth remaineth, seedtime and harvest, summer and winter shall not fail.

Thrashing by hand, though for some years out of date, is now coming into fashion again: so at least I was told as I stood watching two of Farmer Pinmarsh's men wielding their flails opposite each other, on the boarded space between the doors of the tithe barn. They stayed their rhythmic swing to explain that 'a smart few maisters has bee-uns flailed nowadays, 'cause if they be put through the machine the straw gets that bruk about, it ben't o' much use on fur the ship.' They begged me politely, to try my skill with the flail, assuring me that it was 'easy anuff to do when onst arra-one wur usted to 't.' I declined the offer, being mindful of an evil reputation this agricultural instrument enjoys for flying round and dealing the amateur thrasher a shrewd and unexpected crack upon the head. The barn in which the two men were working was that wherein the parson used formerly to store his tithe (hence its name) when this was paid in kind. There is a story current in

12

HAND FLAILING

the village that a certain woman – the mother of nine – heard of the rector's claim to a tenth part of the livestock, and on the arrival of her next infant she promptly had it conveyed to the parsonage as her contribution to his income! Seeing however that she refused to tithe aught more profitable than her own children, the baby was returned. In another case the clergy-man actually did adopt the tenth child of a parishioner, and brought up and educated the boy at his own expense.

The tithe barn is a noble building, long and lofty, having two sets of double doors that project like a porch, and a high-pitched timbered roof. These great barns are a feature of the district, and were built for the storage of the corn which is grown about here so largely. The majority are made of tarred or painted planks overlapping one another, and are provided with wide entrances capable of admitting a loaded wagon or the box of a thrashing machine. Opposite these doors are others giving access to the farmyard, and between them is a stretch of boarded floor – the rest of the barn being paved with bricks – where thrashing by flail, winnowing and chaff cutting are carried on. The two last employments are particu-larly distasteful to the men. Winnowing necessitates a draught and is regarded as an infallible recipe for the acquisition of colds, 'the rheumatiz,' 'brantitus,' and other kindred evils. Chaff cutting, though not attended by this disadvantage, is

laborious work, involving a heavy strain on certain muscles. Despite the fact that it often means higher pay, good wives begin to feel aggrieved and to talk of the injury to their hus-bands' health if the latter are kept at it longer than three months running, and soldier sons write home from abroad – as I have read – to say: 'I was very glad to hear that father don't go to chaff cutting now, for it is very hard work and tiring, and I shold be very glad if I was 'im.'

Eleanor Hayden

THE CARRIER

In spite of the march of civilisation, the old carrier's cart still haunts our highways. It is true that some of our carriers have launched out and started motor-wagons, but the old-fashioned cart, with its large hood, or the covered light wagon drawn by a horse that has seen better days and is rather gone at the knees, is still with us, and its owner is a useful member of our village community. He is a link with the civilization of our nearest town, the purveyor of news, the conveyer of divers goods, and the welcome gossip of every cottage and every ser-vants' hall. He is an exceedingly leisurely individual, and stops

13

BRACKNELL

innumerable times at the various houses on his route, discharging countless commissions.

The carriers have their special stations at an inn in the county town, the 'Black Horse' or the 'Red Lion,' where you will always find their carts drawn up in line during the day, until they begin their leisurely journey homewards. It is a curious life, the carrier's existence; but it must have its attractions for a philosophic mind or for one who loves his fellow-creatures. He has always the companionship of his horse, and perhaps his dog, who guards his van while he is transacting his many errands; and not infrequently he carries human freight, some women gossips who like to do their own shopping and who din into his ear all the latest village news and their opinions upon local affairs and politics. A journey might be undertaken with less cheery and amusing companions.

Peter Ditchfield

FARMING IN THE VALE

The Vale was a decidedly old-fashioned part of England, and not in the least ashamed of being old-fashioned. The village pastimes of wrestling and back-sword play were kept up there perhaps as long as in any portion of middle England. The Childrey schoolmaster, when he was a boy at Uffington, could throw all his schoolfellows. There was an old man at Ardington, somewhat bent and bowlegged, whose shins were deeply scarred from kicks which he had received when his opponents 'played rough' in wrestling; but back-sword play had ceased for some time, as the breaking of heads was too dangerous an amusement. Tom Hughes's description of back-sword at the scouring of the White Horse in 1857 shows how savagely it could be done. The ploughing and harvesting still remained on many farms much the same as it had been one hundred years ago. The soil was in places so heavy that three horses were needed for a plough, and this entailed a carter's boy to lead the front horse, the *plough-boy*, now almost an extinct species of labourer. These poor little fellows had a heavy task, plodding for hours up and down the fields with nothing to vary the monotony of their work. If they were so unfortunate as to lead for an ill-tempered carter they were sure of abuse and perhaps blows if they did not keep the horse up to his work or were clumsy at bringing him round when the headland was reached. Oxen for ploughing had nearly disappeared, though Sir William Throckmorton still used them at Buckland, near Faringdon, and Farmer Rebbeck, of Kingston Lisle, had a team. He had even trained a fine young bull for

working, which I saw one day drawing a harrow wisely and well. I got into conversation with the man who tended him and heard that the bull was 'all right with his work, only you marn't bet he'.

When harvest time came most of the villagers migrated to the cornfields, for in 1883 nearly all the wheat and most of the barley was cut by hand. The fields were usually about one furlong wide, and perhaps there might be eight acres of wheat ready for cutting and, let us say, eight men engaged on the task. They would draw lots for their strips in the field, and then eight families would begin to drive their pathways into the standing corn. I said eight *families*, though perhaps some of the men who were 'widow men', i.e., bachelors, must work alone and be so outdistanced by their more fortunate neighbours.

Father, with his broad-bladed fagging hook in his right hand and crooked stick in his left, slashed through the yellow stalks and left them gathered by his foot. Mother followed, swept a sheaf together, placed it on 'the bond', drew this lightly and fastened it by a twist. The children pulled the bonds, the younger perhaps only able to select the six or eight stalks needed to make one, the elder making them ready for mother to use.

I never acquired the knack of twisting a bond, which is made by placing three or four ears of corn across one another and turning the stalks so that the ears somehow interlock and pull against each other so strongly that even when the corn has been stacked and the threshing machine is at work the man on

MARTHA AND FRANCIS DYER, BRIMPTON

THE GEORGE AND DRAGON, SWALLOWFIELD

the rick who feeds the machine must cut through the encircling bond before he sends the sheaf down the shoot. That it is a triumph of simple skill in using material is evident when we count up all the strains which the bond has to endure: first when it is drawn round the sheaf and the end tucked in tightly; next when the sheaf is placed in the shocks; again when pitched on to the wagon; a fourth time as the wagon is unloaded at the stack; finally when lifted for threshing.

Heavy crops of barley were 'fagged' with the broadhook and gathered in sheaves, but light crops on hillsides would be mown with the scythe and left to dry on the ground. The men drew lots for their places in the first field, and the rule was 'As you fall out so you fall in', which, being interpreted, means that the first man who finished his strip in field number one took the first lot in field number two. This rule saved much grumbling, for a section of the cornfield might be 'laid', and so entail extra labour in the cutting of the corn, or another strip in the field might be 'a poor plant' and easy to clear. But since 'Us drawed cuts for he', no one had a right to grumble at the luck of his neighbour.

From some of the older farm-hands I learned of the reaping of wheat, then so precious, with sickles. The wheat was cut about the height of a man's knee and long stubble remained in the field. The reason for this was that the wheat would be stacked in the great barns and so the sheaves were made small

and the space in the barns economized. The reaping of the wheat was done by gathering in the left hand a number of stalks and then slicing them with the sickle. A good workman could make a full-sized sheaf with three handfuls of wheat. Sickles had not been used for a long time, but one saw them occasionally hung up in cottages, for the old custom was to bind them up with tape after harvest so to keep them sharp and free from rust till next year. Sickles, which Berkshire folk often called shekels, are narrow in the blade, very light, and have a toothed edge. Though now almost unknown in English farming, they are still made in Yorkshire for export to all parts of the world.

The many years of plenty for the farmers and landowners had ceased in 1883, but one heard much about those times when corn and wool fetched such high prices and labour was so plentiful and cheap. In the 'sixties many of the tenants who rented large farms under good landlords made great profits, and not a few of them saved money steadily. Even in the 'seventies many were still thriving. 'I never can put by two thousand a year', one of them said to his Parson in a moment of confidence. 'They did not have to make money, it was brought home and shot down at their doors,' was a remark I heard later when it was most difficult to make farming pay. It was like the good times in Suffolk on a more lavish scale. The contrast between the lot of the owners and farmers on the one hand

16

UFFINGTON

and the labourers on the other was too great; for bread and sugar and tea were all dear. Most pathetic were the reminiscences of the older men and women about the baked crusts which mother put into the teapot, and the packet of sugar which was bought as a treat, but 'the rain soaked the paper as I came back from Wantage and almost all of it ran out'. The carter boys on lonely farms lived in a 'cot' during the week and carried from home their supply of bread and lard, as well as sugar and tea, if they could afford any. 'The air on the Downs made one hungry and I often finished my bread on Friday night and had none till I got my wages on Saturday', said one elderly man.

If a farmer and his wife were kind-hearted they would help their men, perhaps allowing them to buy a sack of wheat cheaply and pay for it by instalments; but not all farmers were kind, and not all of them rented from wise landlords. The competition for farms pushed up rents too fast, and many a landlord also insisted on maintaining too large a head of game. They would not allow a hare or rabbit to be shot, and ground game thrives on chalk hill land. Sometimes the landlords themselves did not know how much damage was being done, as the following story will show.

One week there appeared in a Berks paper a letter about the devastation of a great cornfield which surrounded a small wood. 'We name no names,' of course, but the owner recognized the description and said to his tenant (who had not written the letter): 'I know it means your field; have the dam-

LETCOMBE REGIS

17

WANTAGE TRAMWAY

ALMSWOMAN, WANTAGE

age estimated and I will pay you, in full.' The tenant thanked him cordially, and the landlord, a man justly well liked, went home with a feeling of virtuous satisfaction. But he was less happy when in a few days the valuer sent him an estimate for £120; and his keepers had orders to thin the rabbits and hares drastically. Everyone knows what a plague rabbits can be, but the damage from too many hares on a sheep farm is not common knowledge. They have a bad habit of nibbling a bit from several turnips instead of making a meal off one, and then each turnip may begin to decay. Moreover, they are a prolific species, for the doe may have two litters of leverets in a year, and sometimes the early leverets have a litter before they are a year old. 'There were more hares than sheep on my farm,' said a man to me when telling of the times when his landlord was too particular about the game.

James Cornish

COUNTRY CLOTHES

Dress in the country was very plain, but good of its kind. All women wore long skirts, and as soon as they married wore neat little bonnets – not hats. My grandmother always wore white stockings and elastic sided boots. When I first remember her she was not 50 (for my mother married at 19), but even then she wore a lace cap with a little bit of black velvet in the front, and in the winter she always wore a woollen cross-over shawl. She never wore anything but black, with a very full skirt.

18

FOX AND HOUNDS, WALTHAM

Farmers wore breeches, gaiters and boots, and very smart they looked, and for riding they wore a square-shaped bowler hat.

Women's dresses were most elaborate to make. They were lined, were very full in the skirt, which was turned up with braid to give extra strength as they were long enough to sweep the ground. The bodice of the dress was high up to the neck, and had little bones to keep it up, sometimes as high as the ears! White frilling was often used as a neck finish, and looked neat and nice. Some bodices were tight-fitting and had quantities of small buttons all down the front. Waists were small, and young ladies wanting to be extra smart wore bustles.

Under the skirt numerous petticoats were worn, one of them always a red flannel one, at least in the winter. We used to scallop and embroider white flannel ones for the children. Aprons were always worn by grown-ups and very pretty silk and satin ones were worn over their afternoon dresses by older married women.

Children always wore pinafores. Plain ones for the nursery or schoolroom, and very elaborate ones for coming down to the drawing room after tea. These were made of nainsook, tucked and embroidered.

The most amusing dress of all that I can remember from my young days was the *bathing-dress*. We always went to the seaside for a holiday in the summer; Bournemouth or the Isle of Wight were the usual places, I suppose because they were easy to get to – by train, of course. Before we left home we were

all fitted out with bathing gowns made by our visiting dressmaker. They were made of navy blue serge, and took simply yards of material. They went up to the neck, and finished there with a frill, the trousers came to the ankles and were gathered into a band there – I suppose in case a bit of leg should show! The bodice was a loose, blousey sort of thing, buttoned down the front; and when the bather had got into this voluminous garment, she fixed round her waist a deep frill, which went all the way round the body, and down to the knees. The suit was trimmed with white, or red braid, so did not look quite so funereal as it sounds, but face, hands and feet were the only parts of the body uncovered!

The bathing, too, was wonderful. You took your ticket at a little hut on the beach, and were shown into an empty bathing machine down near the sea. The old bathing woman (they were always fat!) told you to bolt the door and let her know when you were ready. You began to undress and then to your surprise the machine began to move and jerked and creaked and rolled from side to side. A horse had been hooked on to the front of it and had drawn you into the sea! (So lookers-on could not even see bare feet!) The old bathing woman was waiting for you and told you to take hold of the rope fixed to the machine and not to leave go of it.

Can you picture a country child, on her first visit to the sea, gingerly going down the three or four steps into the sea, and then afraid to go to the end of the rope. Of course we soon got used to it, and had great fun, bobbing up and down, and

19

SULHAM FARM

playing in the water, but unfortunately the boys could not join us. The sexes must be kept a long way apart, so they had to go to the men's machines at the other end of the beach.

I believe it was in the Isle of Wight that two old ladies bought a house on the cliff. When the bathing season started they were horrified to find that the men's machines were not quite out of sight from their windows. They protested to the agent, who said, 'Madam, your sight must be very good, for I cannot see whether they are men or women!' 'Oh!' was the answer, 'but I use the glasses!'

Mourning was a gruesome thing in Victoria's time. After Prince Albert died, she wore black for the rest of her life, and all widows did the same. I know my mother never wore colours again after my father died.

It was the custom for any near relative to wear all black with crepe trimmings for a year, the second year black and white, mauve and grey. Even small children were put into black. Adults had handkerchiefs with half an inch of black round the edges, and notepaper the same, but as the months went by that became narrower until only a very narrow black edge remained.

When Queen Victoria died everybody went into mourning; the gloom was dreadful. In church, for instance, to see nothing but a crowd of black objects was most depressing. That public mourning did not last very long. People were told in the newspapers when they could leave it off.

Funerals, too, were terrible things. For anyone of any importance there was a hearse with four black horses. The horses had black plumes standing from their bridles, and black cloths hanging down on each side of them. Men walked by the side of the hearse in black morning coats, and top hats with a long black veil hanging down the back. The mourners followed in closed carriages at the slowest possible walking pace, and the bell tolled all the time. Friends or acquaintances wishing to show respect, who possessed carriages, sent them to the funeral to represent themselves. That is to say if they had a coachman to drive the carriage, for nobody would ride in those complimentary carriages. Fortunately, except for a very near relative, women and girls were not expected to attend the funeral. By the time I had to attend a funeral I am glad to say it was customary to have flowers, and things were a little less gloomy.

It has always been the custom in the country, and still is, for the relatives bereaved to attend a church service on the Sunday after the funeral. They may never go to church at any other time, or be chapel goers, or atheists, but they always go then. There must, I think, be some superstition attached to this practice, but I have never been able to find the reason.

Jane Taylor

20

BOARD OF GUARDIANS' MEETING ROOM, WOKINGHAM WORKHOUSE

A VISIT TO READING WORKHOUSE

Sir,

I have so often heard the hope expressed by elderly people tht they might be carried to their grave in preference to the Workhouse that I determined when opportunity offered to pay it a visit to ascertain what grounds their fears were built upon and by invitation of a member of the Board and the courtesy of the estimable master (Mr Pope) my wish was gratified last Wednesday, early closing day. I had no idea of the extensive character of the institution, which occupied $1\frac{1}{2}$ hours in active inspection. Everything was so spick and span (so clean and in such good order) that credit is due to the managing authority. I was specially pleased with the visit to the aged (male and female) wards, and to see the smile of pleasure which greeted the master as he made the kindly enquiry, 'Are you alright here?' Several familiar faces I noted amongst them, and though I could not but regret their presence I was pleased to receive their assurance of being well-cared for. I noted a great improvement in one called 'John' whom I knew as a regular attendant at Coley Hall. The old ladies too, in their caps, print dresses, etc., looked and felt (as they assured me) very much at home round their cosy fire. Some were engaged in sewing, others in reading.

I also visited the sick and imbecile wards. The former had every comfort, and the latter had similar surroundings, and were doubtless as much so as their melancholy state permitted. In the latter I saw a man very familiar to us about the town with a tray of cakes upon his head, who I was told by Mr Pope had been much given to the game of 'tossing'. I was told to make a motion by placing my fingers in my palm in imitation of that vicious habit, and doing so he immediately cried, 'heads'. I gave him a penny, which produced a smile well worth the outlay. One of the inmates with a ruby proboscis said he would devote a penny if given to him to purchasing a glass of ale, and if two were given to him he would do ditto. I was also shown the oakum, and the quantity given to tramps to pick in payment for their supper, bed and breakfast, and I honestly believe supper time would come round again before I could complete it, but Mr Pope assured me some of them did it with ease. I saw one man doing punishment in the shape of stonebreaking, and from the way he was puffing over the job I believe the lesson will be salutary.

HUNTLEY AND PALMERS BISCUIT FACTORY, READING

I was much interested in the cell for refractory inmates, where in lieu of a window a large projecting sieve is put in which projects like a summer blind and through which all the stones have to be thrown (when small enough) which have been allotted them to break as a punishment. I also visited the kitchen which was a marvel of cleanliness and order; saw the bread and butter for tea and the slices of bread and cheese for supper. I also inspected and found it sufficient in quantity and of excellent quality, the bread being very fine. Much more might be written of the excellent arrangements for wood chopping and other work, but your space is too valuable.

I should like to add that the only fault I can find is that only once a month out is allowed. It should be altered to once a week, or at all events liberty might be given to any gentleman to take a batch of the old men out in the country for a stroll, say on Wednesday afternoons, and to any lady (so kindly disposed) to be chaperone to the old ladies. It would be a great delight to them and give real pleasure to those undertaking the duty. I would gladly do so once a month.

Thanking the members of the Board for the favour and Mr Pope for his courtesy, and hoping it may be a long time before it is necessary to elect a new Pope in the place of him who reigns over them in so kindly a manner and with such great ability,

I am, etc.,
'Wanderer'

Reading Observer, April 2 1892

AMUSING RACE AT THE PALMER PARK

On Saturday afternoon a most amusing race took place on the Palmer Park track, the contestants being Jack Barker, a man of forty-seven, who is employed in the box room at the Biscuit Factory, and Albert Walters, a young man of eighteen, employed in the packing room at the Biscuit Factory. For some time keen rivalry has existed between the two, and their partizans were anxious that the two should have a trial of strength. Accordingly, it was arranged that, for a substantial stake, the two should meet at three o'clock at the Palmer Park on Saturday, the distance to be run being one mile. The contestants, each accompanied by a band of supporters, arrived at the park about two o'clock. Of course, the long and tedious process of priming them up had to be gone through, and this necessitated an early arrival. Barker was well rubbed down with onion, but the task of preparing Walters for the great event was a more arduous one. Peppermint, onions, lemons, and machine oil were applied, and a scrubbing brush was brought into requisition, so that the ingredients should be properly rubbed in. Much interest centered round the event, and there was a large crowd when the two men turned out to take their places. At the given signal the two started off. Barker led from the first lap, but it was soon apparent that he was no match for the younger man, who went ahead, and won easily by twelve yards, in 6 min., amid the cheers of his supporters. The usual speechifying followed. The winner made a short speech, being prompted by some of his friends. At the conclu-

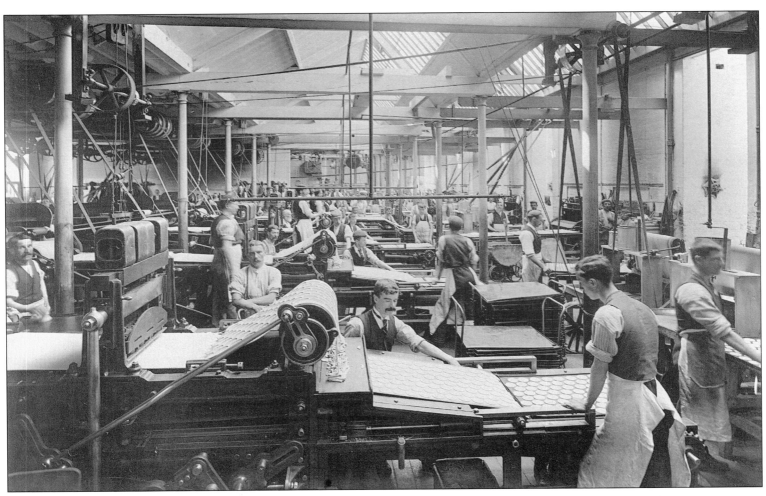

HUNTLEY AND PALMERS BISCUIT FACTORY, READING

sion of his oration there were loud cries for Barker. The older man attributed his defeat to lack of training, and said he had of late been suffering from erysipelas and blood poisoning. The two men then shook hands, and the parties adjourned to the dressing room, where it was decided to hold another race, in a month's time, over a distance of two miles, the younger man to concede two hundred yards. This over, a procession was formed, and headed by the two men, the party proceeded along London Road. A truck was procured, and Walters, whose jacket was covered with rosettes, was placed in it. Barker preferred to walk. A halt was made by the Corporation lamp near the Cemetery, around which the Salvation Army were holding a meeting, and the winner made a short speech. The party then broke up. The affair was nothing but a hoax, and was much enjoyed by its promoters.

Berkshire Chronicle, 5 May 1892

PICTURES OF BLEWBURY

Right in the village of Blewbury stands a red-brick house. It is a very ordinary-looking little house, yet it has received a good deal of attention, not for the sake of itself, but for its swinging sign. Now, in this twentieth century, if any man had ventured to

paint such a sign, I feel quite sure that every woman, even in the remote village of Blewbury, would have felt that she owed it as a duty to her sex to make it what is commonly called 'too hot' for him. Certainly he would not have dared to show his face when once that sign had been exposed to view. It is called the 'Load of Mischief,' and the Load of Mischief is a woman; the bearer of the burden a man, presumably her husband. This woman, a most disagreeable virago, is sitting 'piggyback' upon the man's shoulders in company with a monkey and a magpie – the moral evidently intended being that a woman, a monkey, and a magpie are all equally troublesome and mischievous, and to be avoided. In her hand the woman holds a glass of gin, in the background of the picture is a public-house called 'Cuckhold's Fortune', on the right-hand side the pawnshop of S. Gripe, which a carpenter is entering to pledge his tools. The original of this curious design, which hangs upon an old inn in London, is said to be by Hogarth, and to be mentioned in the lease of the house as one of the fixtures; how the replica found its way to Blewbury is a mystery, and we will not insult the Blewburians by imagining for one moment that the model for its unpleasant heroine was discovered in their midst.

However, upon other occasions the inhabitants of the village have formed subjects for pictures, the result proving not always satisfactory to the models. This was the case, at any rate, in one memorable instance. The artist had painted two old

23

TOWN HALL AND CROWN INN, FARINGDON

bodies talking over a cottage garden gate. The fact of being painted pleased them well enough, and all went well until the picture was exhibited in London. 'The Gossips,' the name of the picture, presently reached the old ladies' ears, but when it was too late to alter it; their indignation at being, as they considered, so maligned, was immense.

Luke Fildes found the models for his 'Village Wedding' in Blewbury. It was, in fact, a real country wedding party, and the members of it were doubtless immensely flattered at 'having their likenesses took,' although the poor bridegroom endured great discomfort during the operation. His face grew whiter and whiter, and the artist inquired at last if he were not feeling well. 'I do find it such a job a 'olding of my breath,' he burst out, with an explosion of relief at being able to speak. His only experience of portraiture had been a cheap daguerreotype [an early photographic technique], during the taking of which, to ensure perfect immobility, he had been told to hold his breath.

L.S.

THE BLIND HOUSE

A picturesque building is the old Town Hall of Faringdon, standing in the Market Place with the Crown Inn at its side.

The latter was the Court House in times gone by for the trial of prisoners. In a corner of the building under the same roof as the Town Hall was a small cell called the Blind House, a dismal little place lighted only by a few bars of grating over the door – hence its name. The prisoners incarcerated in the Blind House, awaiting the coming of the magistrates, must have spent the time in somewhat cramped positions, the space being extremely limited. Their friends did their utmost to ameliorate their misfortunes by squeezing packets of tobacco and eatables through the bars of the prison. These sympathetic people outside had also an ingenious device lest the inmates of the Blind House should chance to suffer from thirst. The bowl end of a long clay pipe was inserted into a pot of beer. The other end found its way into the mouth owned by a thirsty soul inside the cell, the prisoners standing in turn upon the lock of the door in order to reach the refreshing draught. Much squabbling must have gone on over that friendly pipe, and some difference of opinion as to when each turn had come to an end, or perhaps – who knows? – there was honour among thieves, and the whole thing was arranged amicably.

Just outside the door of the Blind House the stocks were set up, and the passers-by were treated to glowering looks from the prisoners in them. In most villages the stocks were placed just outside the church gate in order that the righteous glances of the churchgoers might have the effect of still more putting the delinquents to shame. A primitive idea of punishment, this

FARINGDON CATTLE MARKET

idea of openly shaming wrong-doers; harmless, perhaps, but not very elevating either for the spectators or for those who were looked at.

'If they were put in the stocks when the people went into church there they had to stop till 'em came out again,' an old man told me. He himself, so the story goes, had been the last man to occupy the stocks in Faringdon. But as to this occurrence he maintained a rigid silence – 'Oh, yes, he remembered the stocks well enuf' – but nothing more. The lapse of time I thought might have invested the situation with some humour in his eyes – turned it, in fact, into a huge joke. I was grievously mistaken.

L.S.

THE FOLLY AND THE WHITE HORSE

There are two things which you will hear constantly mentioned at Faringdon; with the name of one of them you will be already familiar, the other will probably be new to you. The first is the White Horse Hill, the second is the Folly.

'Give me the fresh air of the White Horse Hill, London's too smoky; it is not healthy'; the pride of possession inspires the words; one likes to hear them, just as one likes to hear it said over and over again when the weather is especially beautiful: 'Ah, it must be fine up on White Horse Hill to-day; this is the sort of day to be on White Horse Hill.' It makes one realise all that the White Horse Hill means to those people whose families for generations past have lived within touch and sight of it – how it is part of themselves; woven into the woof of their existence.

But the Folly. When I first went to Faringdon the Folly was not even so much as a name to me. 'You must go and see the Folly; you will like that.' No one told me what I was going to see. So I climbed the hill to the Folly, and found that it was nothing more, and nothing less, than a group of isolated fir trees, upon an eminence which forms a landmark to all the country round. Wonderful fir trees they are – of great height, with huge trunks and spreading tops. The lower branches are nearly all gone, pulled off doubtless for firewood. I know how it is done. As I came up the hill there were three little girls and a bigger boy all busily engaged in this mischief. The boy threw a noose over the branch, almost now the only one within

FARINGDON

reach; then he and the three little girls hung upon the rope and pulled. A few minutes longer, a little more pulling, and the branch would have been broken. But I appeared upon the scene. I begged them to desist, which they did, only probably till my back was turned. That branch, I felt sure, was doomed; the children would return to their work of destruction, and all my protestations be wasted.

The grove of fir trees is round, like a crown upon the top of the hill. Underneath the trees you walk over the most deliciously soft turf, cropped just closely enough to be pleasant to the feet. Here much courting goes on; the place is made for it. There are rough seats, and a path has been cut right across the grass and another round the hill. And the hills misty and grey by reason of their distance. Upon a clear day

The snow-white courser stretching o'er the green

is indistinctly visible – that is, if you know just where to look for it. For all the rest embraced by that wonderful panoramic view I must refer you to the effusion called 'Faringdon Hill,' by Henry James Pye, Poet Laureate, of whom more hereafter. For myself, shall I make this confession? – I had no wish or any desire whatever for anything so prosaic as to know the names of the places within my sight. The view itself, the grey hills and the beautiful country in between, was enough. It would have afforded me absolutely no satisfaction to know that from the Folly I could see seven counties, or twelve, or even twenty. For while I sat upon one of those benches, very

uncomfortably, as far as physical ease was concerned, I made a discovery, or rather a revelation came to me. The air was full of twitterings; above my head in the fir trees a couple of wood-pigeons cooed continually. I became sensible of an indescribable vibration thrilling through Nature, a restlessness and movement, an eager stirring of suppressed life. And suddenly I knew that it all meant. The spring had come; it had come, too, actually a whole day in advance of the calendar.

Yesterday was Saturday. I had longed with such an intense longing for warmth and the sunshine; but the wind had howled louder and moaned more sadly than ever before. Now this is only Sunday, and the sky is blue – the blue of a turquoise. Yesterday there were stifled sobs; a wearied-out patience with the long, long winter. To-day all Creation is laughing and stretching out its hands towards happiness as towards a right. Now all is clear, for nothing but fruition can explain the seed-time, otherwise there would be no meaning in patience and hope. And whether spring and the fulfilment of hope comes early or tarries long, every flake of snow, every storm of rain, each bitter wind, all the sadness of winter which is bound up in the eternal purpose must first be accomplished. Then, and not one moment sooner, will the spring be here. At this point my reflections were interrupted by a voice behind me: 'Well, that's a rum sort o' game, that is.' Looking round, I found that the remark proceeded from an old man; the game he referred to was the game of golf, which was being played by a man and a girl in the fields below the hill. I do not know how long the old man had been standing behind

WHITE HORSE HILL

me. I suppose his conclusion was the result of some minutes' observation. But really, now that my attention was drawn to it, I felt very much inclined to agree with him. Viewed from a distance – by the uninitiated, shall I say? – golf, *is* a very 'rum sort o' game'; rather, the difficulty lies in believing it is a 'game' at all. The girl stoops down and puts something upon the ground. There is a great deal of preliminary swinging of a stick or club, then one final swing, with no result whatever apparently, for if you are watching the game for the first time and from a distance you are probably not made aware that these mighty efforts are directed towards the precipitating into space of a tiny ball about the size of an egg. Then the man stoops, raises himself, and goes through the same blandishments, with the same exhibition of gigantic effort of strength. This being accomplished the pair start off, walk for some distance, stop, and go through the same pantomime over again. It did look a very 'rum sort o' game'. I was not surprised at the contemptous decision of a group of lads who had also stopped near me to watch, that they should 'prefer football'. Golf was perhaps a novel sensation to the Faringdonians.

But the pride they feel in their hill is no novel sensation to them. The sentiment expressed by the old man as he walked beside me down the path that he 'shouldn't think there was another such hill in the kingdom', is probably largely the feeling amongst the natives of the little Berkshire town. They do not take its existence altogether as a matter of course either; if you question them on the subject you will find they have theories about it. Much mystery surrounds the Folly. There are many traditions and stories connected with it, the most

obviously impossible one being that a member of the Pye family, once great folk at Faringdon, planted a tree of it every day! 'There goes Pye and his Folly' the people are reported to have said as Mr Pye was seen going up the hill upon his daily mission. The story may have some foundation in fact; it certainly possesses no connection with the Folly. The Pyes only came to Faringdon in 1621, and there is extant an old picture of Faringdon in 1630, in which the trees of the Folly appear to be almost as tall as they are now. The clump crowning Jasper's Hill, another height not far from the Folly, which was cut down about thirty years ago, also appears in the picture. No; we must go farther back than this: the mystery surrounding the Folly is not so easily swept away. The suggestion that the origin of the name is simply *folium* certainly does not dispose of it. Long ago, ages before Alfred fought his battles, before even this bit of country formed part of the habitable world, there was perhaps a great forest here, of which this glorious group of trees alone remains. The supposition only deepens the mystery. And the pride of the Faringdon folk in their Folly is justified and comprehensible.

L.S.

POACHERS

The poacher can be very cunning and has a wonderful sly discretion. A new-comer to the neighbourhood was walking over his newly purchased fields, accompanied by his dogs, and

WEST ILSLEY

found some rabbit snares, cunningly devised wires with a slip noose. He made quite a collection of them and put them into his pocket. Meeting an innocent-looking man, well known in the district as a very skilful poacher, though his prowess was unknown to the gentleman, he showed him the wires, and said:

'See what I have found in my fields. What are these curious wires for?'

The man looked at them, pretended to examine them with care and curiosity, and then after humming and hemming a little, he said:

'I 'specks they be collars for your little dogs, sir,' an explanation which the gentleman seemed to think quite reasonable.

Peter Ditchfield

OLD ROGER

A children's game in which the players form a ring, hand in hand, one child lies down in the centre (Roger) and another (old woman) stands a little distance away.
The children sing:

> Old Roger is dead and he lies in his grave,
> lies in his grave, lies in his grave.

> Old Roger is dead and he lies in his grave,
> Heigh! ho! lies in his grave.

> There hangs an old apple tree over his head,
> over his head, over his head.
> There hangs an old apple tree over his head,
> Heigh! ho! over his head.

> The apples were ripe and ready to fall,
> ready to fall, ready to fall.
> The apples were ripe and ready to fall,
> Heigh! ho! ready to fall.

The 'old woman' enters the ring and pretends to pick up apples.

> There came an old woman a picking them up,
> picking them up, picking them up.
> There came an old woman a picking them up,
> Heigh! ho! picking them up.

'Old Roger' jumps up and gives her a push.

> Old Roger jumped up and he gave her a knock,
> gave her a knock, gave her a knock.
> Old Roger jumped up and he gave a knock
> Heigh! ho! gave her a knock.

BISHAM

The 'old woman' hobbles out of the ring.

Which made the old woman go hippety hop,
hippety hop, hippety hop.
Which made the old woman go hippety hop,
Heigh! ho! hippety hop.

Emma Thoyts (Old Berkshire School Games, c. 1890)

MRS PINMARSH'S SYLLABUB

To Mrs Pinmarsh's hay-parties only children were invited. The chief feature of the entertainment was a syllabub which she prepared herself from one of her old recipes. After tea and games among the hay, the little visitors were seated in a half-circle, and each was supplied with a saucer and a spoon. Every eye would then be turned in the direction of the yard, whence ere long Mrs Pinmarsh would be seen coming towards the field, bearing a large china bowl, and various other impedimenta. Behind her solemnly marched the fogger leading the best cow – the one, that is, which gave the richest milk. The procession halted on the chord of the half-circle, and the rite commenced amid profound silence. Into the bowl was turned a bottle of home-brewed ale, deemed by the careful hostess

more suited to youthful consumers than red or white wine. Then came sugar, white and sparkling, and as fine as sifting could make it; nutmeg followed, grated while the guests looked on, and now there remained but to add the crowning glory. While the fogger – quite needlessly – held the quiet animal, that gazed about her mildly with a wondering eye, Mrs Pinmarsh drew the sweet warm milk, until it frothed high in the bowl. The syllabub was ladled into saucers thrust forth by impatient hands, and, the ceremony ended, the cow was led back to the yard to resume her ordinary routine until hay time came round again.

Eleanor Hayden

HARVEST HOME

When 'all was safely gathered in' then came the Harvest Home supper. In some villages the thanksgiving in church would be on a week-day afternoon and be followed by the feast, but gradually that died out and the church festival was held on a Sunday.

On an appointed day one end of the barn was cleared of winnowing machine, root pulper, chaff cutter and sacks, etc., etc., then swept and tidied; trestle tables and forms (usually

THE GREEN, DRAYTON

EAST HENDRED

borrowed from the chapel) were brought in; all the hurricane lanterns on the farm were collected and cleaned. We children loved the bustle of preparation and ran about trying to help but probably getting in the way and hindering!

The tables were covered with strips of new, unbleached calico, and lighted by candles, whose soft light reflected kindly on the honest, toil-worn faces of the guests. The hurricane lanterns hung on nails round the walls added a little more light to the great vaulted barn, but this only served to make the other end of the barn look very dark and eerie; and you can guess we children kept as far away from that as we could!

The workers and their wives, all in Sunday best and faces polished with soap and water, arrived punctually at six o'clock, and waited outside until invited in. The vicar said grace, and thanked God for the blessing of the harvest and the bountiful repast – then the meal started.

At one end of the tables was a huge joint of hot roast beef, carved by my father. This was served on the pewter 'well' dish (how well I remember this dish!). It was a terrific weight to carry, because it had boiling water underneath to keep the joint hot, and under the meat there were little ditches to carry the gravy down to the 'well' at the end, where it could be spooned up with a giant gravy spoon.

The other end of the table had a joint of lovely pink *salt* beef, which was of course boiled. This was surrounded on its dish by onions, carrots and turnips; and at intervals down the tables were bowls of potatoes and cabbage.

DONNINGTON CASTLE FARM

When plateful after plateful had disappeared, in came the 'gurt big figgetty puddens' – the old Berkshire name for plum duff, or 'spotted Dick'.

The waitresses were a visitor or two, and the farmhouse maids, who looked neat and pretty in dainty cotton frocks and muslin aprons and caps.

A neighbour was kept busy the whole evening 'drawing' beer from the big 18-gallon cask put up in the barn a few days before. This beer, brewed at a local brewery a few miles away, was wonderful stuff, made of wholesome malt and hops, and it cost 6d. a gallon! How this good old ale would blush with shame at having to share the same name as the feeble fluid of today! There is no doubt that it played a great part in making the yeomen of England the sturdy craftsmen they were, and as they were fond of saying, 'This warms the cockles of your heart all right'!

Next it was the turn of the clay pipes to be filled with strong 'shag' tobacco put out on saucers down the table; and soon the barn was as misty inside as the autumn night outside the big doors.

When the tables were finally cleared, and silence reigned – there was little or no talking – my father would say 'Now for a song, who'll make a start?' *Dead* silence! Then a nudge or two and a whispered, 'Go on, you!' and without any warning, still sitting and with eyes cast down, Joe or Bill would suddenly burst into song; and for the rest of the evening there was no pause in the rush of song.

Everbody seemed to know all the words and joined in all the choruses. The correct procedure was for the soloist to sing the chorus *after each verse*, and *then* the audience. I remember one song had twelve verses, so this made thirty-six verses altogether!

The 'Farmer's Boy' was always one of the chosen songs, but the majority were about red-coated soldier boys dying, far away in a foreign land. There was one called 'Bingen on the Rhine', in which the young soldier is writing to the 'dear old mother' at home. Another exciting one that we liked told of the girl who married another. The chorus went:

WINDSOR REGATTA

'She was false and deceitful, cold-hearted young girl – let her go!'

The last bit, '*let her go*', being literally yelled – but how everybody enjoyed it.

There was one they all sang together, something like this:

'Well ploughed, well sowed,
Well reaped, well mowed,
Nar 'a (not a) load overdrawed (tipped over)
Whoop, whoop, Harvest Home.'

I never remember any of the women attempting to sing a solo, but a very popular saying was 'A whistlin' 'ooman and a crowin' hen is neither good for God nor men'. Once the singer started off in rather a high key, there were immediate shouts of 'Come down on to the B, Jarge' – and Jarge did!

I don't remember the actual time of breaking up, but in those days it was always early to bed. An old saying was 'If 'a (he) lays abed marnins, 'a wunt never grow rich'. At last someone would make a move, and then one by one the guests walked past the master and missus, the men touching their forelocks, and the women bobbing a little curtsey. Good night to 'ee, sir; good night, ma'am, and thank 'ee kindly.' As they wandered off down the lane to their little cottage homes lighted by the ever beautiful old 'harvest' moon (or if it was a late

season it would be the 'hunter's' moon), they would probably be thinking, 'Another harvest safely over, now we must begin getting ready for the next'. The countryman in those days was a simple soul with a childlike faith, living day by day in close touch with Nature.

Jane Taylor

WINDSOR DIARY 1887

June 19
Tonight I have been to Langley to preach. On crossing Victoria Bridge I saw a small crowd near the bathing place on the Datchet side & on enquiring found that a soldier had been drowned while bathing and they were just putting in the drags for his dead body. Within a yard or two of the spot at which he sank some youths were still bathing in the most unconcerned manner. How terribly insensible is the unrenewed human heart.

June 20
The Jubilee rejoicings are in full cry. This morning the Queen left Windsor for London to be ready for the celebration at Westminster Abbey tomorrow. The town is gorgeously decorated & when illuminated will be a sight to be remembered.

WINDSOR

This morning a service was held in the Parish Church attended by the Mayor & Corporation in their robes and by representations of the noncomformist bodies. In the Home Park a cricket match was played by the Windsor & District Club *v.* The Yorkshire Gentleman's Club. Prince Christian Victor of Schleswig Holstein was captain of the W & D. This afternoon a troop of Royal Horse Guards (Blue) performed a Musical Ride in the Home Park. The precision of both horses and men in going through the most intricate figures was marvellous. The horses danced to the tune like any human dancer, beating time with their beautiful heads. It was one of the most beautiful sights I ever saw. Tonight a huge bonfire has been burning in in the Home Park. The bonfire was a really grand sight, fed as it was by tar barrels, illuminating in a striking manner the people and the trees. An ox for distribution among the poor has been roasted whole, also in the Home Park. The roasting has not been a great success as the apparatus has not been strong enough. The whole day has been occupied in the operation . . .

June 21
. . . A regatta and aquatic sports have been amongst the sports today. Rather slow, as they usually are in Windsor. The wind-up, however, in the shape of a Venetian fête made up for previous dullness. Hundreds of boats adorned with Chinese lanterns & coloured lamps were lighted up at dark and went in procession up and down the river. The whole concluded with a really magnificent display of fireworks from The Cobbler . . . To add to the effect electric lights & coloured fire were lighted on the Round Tower of the Castle. The town is brilliantly illuminated tonight and crowds of people are in the streets.

June 22
. . . Henry came down this morning to [see] the town decorations and witness the Queen's return to Windsor. The town is thronged with people. Her Majesty arrived at about 7 o'clock this evening and stopped at the bottom of Castle Hill to unveil a statue of herself which has been erected there by the subscriptions of residents in Windsor & District. The statue is of bronze & represents the Queen as in a standing position . . . The likeness is good, it is the work of Boehm, the sculptor . . . When the flag which covered the statue was removed a flourish of trumpets and a roll upon the drums of the Coldstream Guards announced the fact. The Queen gazed earnestly upon the representation of herself, but what her opinion of it was I could not gather from her countenance. I had been waiting in a pew on Castle Hill, but when the Royal Carriage arrived I took the liberty of stepping under the rail into the roadway and had a full view of the Queen's face. A London policeman

NEWBURY RACES

energetically protested but did [not] seem likely to use force, so I quietly retired after I had seen all I wished to see.

June 23
Six thousand children between the ages of 6 and 14 years from the schools of Windsor and a radius of 5 miles around Windsor were entertained to dinner and tea today in the private part of the Home Park. The Queen and several members of her family drove past them as they were drawn up under the trees. About 100 tents put up by the Military accommodated them at dinner & tea.

June 24
Rural sports in the Home Park . . .

June 25
A great Dinner Party at the Castle. Kings and Princes in abundance.

Alexander Elliot

THE MAN WHO TRAINED ROSEBERY

The racing fraternity kept very much to themselves and my acquaintance with them was small, but Mr Clement, of Sparsholt, rented a 'gallop' on the Rectory farm and one day I visited his stables to see the beautiful horses there. His son, who was showing me round, said in quite reverent tones, 'Father trained Rosebery'. By chance I knew of the horse to which he referred, and this is the tale of its amazing success.

Two 'small men' had some racers at Letcombe under Clement's care, and one of the horses, Rosebery by name, was found to be really good. He could go both fast and far and also carry weight. He won several races for them, so they were sure that their swan was not a goose and resolved not to let him appear again for more than a year, but to keep him for the two great Autumn Handicaps at Newmarket, the Cambridgeshire and the Cesarewitch. These two races had never been won by any horse in the same year, for the former was run over a distance of rather more than one mile, and the latter was about twice as far. Yet the owners of Rosebery resolved that he should attempt the apparently impossible. A famous jockey, who was sworn to secrecy and told about their hopes, promised to ride for them in the first race, so they pushed forward with confidence, and to their delight won the Cambridgeshire Stakes. By this victory their horse incurred a penalty of 14 lb., which seemed to make success in the second race quite out of the question, even if Rosebery should be as good a stayer as he was over a mile. 'It never has been done,' said the students of racing form, but the owners and Clement the trainer thought it was going to be done now with their

SEVEN BARROWS, LAMBOURNE

favourite, and they proved to be right. Great were the rejoicings at Letcombe and great were the winnings of all who
backed Rosebery for the double event. It was indeed a triumph of skill in the trainer to prepare a horse so well that he
could win both the long distance and the short distance race
against many of the best in England. Many years passed before
the French mare, Plaisanterie, repeated this feat.

James Cornish

A Solitary Occupation

Among the Downs, a remnant of the past generation still
survives, whom the present age has been unable to modern-
ize save in externals. The greater portion of these men's lives
has been passed in solitude; for weeks at a time they have
been absent from their homes and families, sleeping in a tiny
cot, which was moved from place to place as the require-
ments of the land or the supply of fodder on the ground
necessitated the presence of sheep. An occasional trip to the
nearest village for provisions alone broke the monotony of
their existence during this enforced seclusion, when 'you
med goo fur days wi'out seein' arra-one to spake to, 'ceptin'
'twur yer pooer dog or the ship.' As may be supposed, they
are for the most part a taciturn class, slow of speech, illiter-
ate, incredibly ignorant of the world outside their own limited circuit. One such hermit of the Downs lately mentioned
to his employer the fact that he had never been in a train,
though he had more than once 'sin he a-runnin' along'. The
master, with the kindest intentions, not only gave him a holiday but supplied the funds for an excursion to a distant
town. The 'shuckettin' an' hollerin' of the locomotive
proved too much for the shepherd's nerves: he 'wur that
frowtened,' as he himself expressed it, that on the first available opportunity he descended to *terra firma*, swearing by all

his gods that never again would he commit himself to an
undertaking fraught with such peril as a railway journey.
Despite their ignorance, these old fellows can upon occasion
display a shrewd mother-wit.

'When I wur livin' down in the Vale,' said one who lived
for some years in our village and who may be regarded as a
typical speciment, 'some folks attackted ma, an' med game on
ma, tryin' to put ma in the dark 'cause I wur a shepherd.
"Shepherds be a pooer lot o' iggerants," um sez; "they dwun't
know nothen 'cept 'bout their few ship."

"Have you read your Bible?" sez I to they, "'cause I have,
from Genesis to Revelation, an' I can't see as shepherds be sa
wunnerful little thought on since the beginnin' o' the wor-
ruld. There's Jacob an' Moses an' David as wur shepherds: they
sims to be spoke of ree-speckful anuff in the Bible, by what I
can mek out. An' ther's one thing I'd like to ax 'ee. Have you
iver yeard tell of a carter or a fogger bein' med a king, like
David wur?" Bless 'ee, all them carters and foggers gin up tar-
rifyin' ma fur bein' a shepherd arter that.'

Eleanor Hayden

Jubilee Beacon

We had a thrilling evening at Uffington Castle on the night of
Queen Victoria's Golden Jubilee, June 21st, 1887, when, for
the first time since the Armada, signal beacons were lit all over
England. This was carefully planned and excellently carried
out. The starting place was Malvern Beacon, and the signal a
rocket fired there at 10 p.m. Then every station within sight
was to send up its answering rocket, and no bonfire should be
lit till this had been fired. Mr Butler entrusted the firing of the
rocket to me, and long before dark I had driven my old white
horse, Saxon by name, to the Castle, where many people had
already gathered.

FRIAR STREET, READING

Our beacon was huge and very carefully built in order that it should burn downwards and avoid the obscuring of the flame by smoke. The station south of Malvern to take up the signal was on Cleeve Hill, near Cheltenham, about thirty miles from us, and our rocket was to send on the signal southwards across our Down country to the hills beyond the Kennet Valley. It was a beautiful evening, for Jubilee Day was one of the best of a splendid summer, and I was fascinated in watching the light gradually fading over the wide expanse. No one was quite sure of the exact time, and the minutes crawled slowly till at last I saw a pencil of light far away to the northwest. I shouted to Mr Butler that our signal was seen, and my rocket screeched up into the air. Then came the rush of a scared horse and an angry shout of 'Whatever are you about letting it off like that?' from a farmer who had nearly been unseated. Unluckily for him I recognized his voice: 'Sorry, Mr Frogley', I said, 'but why did you bring a nervous horse here?' Frogley was most apologetic when next we met. 'Fact is I had lumbago and the horse's start hurt me so I could not help crying out.'

Almost before the rocket was down a tall man mounted the ladder and lit the beacon so thoroughly that we feared he would become part of it. The top of the ladder was alight before he came down. Then we could track the line of fires from the Cotswolds to the Chilterns, and looking south over the Downs see those on Highclere, Inkpen and Martinsell Hill till we were tired of counting their number. It was late before I harnessed the horse and drove home to Childrey, taking with me long-enduring memories of a great occasion.

James Cornish

STRONG BEER, FRESH BEER AND SIMS

The ancient inn, with its spreading walnut tree and sturdy, iron-bound stocks nearby, was famed for its generous home-brewed beer. Once I had tasted it and admired its choice flavour, I wanted to know how to make it. To this end I spent an evening with the landlord and he taught me the secret and the whole formula of the trade.

'Many people,' said he, 'use but three things in brewing – malt, hops and water – and of them make three kinds of liquor: strong beer, fresh beer and sims.'

'Strong beer I know, and fresh beer I know, but sims I do not know. What is sims?' I queried.

'It sims like beer, but it isn't,' answered he.

'Then,' said I, quoting an old rhyme that I once heard at harvest home,

'This puts me in mind of Dame Trot when she began to brew
She took half-a-peck of stale malt and half-a-peck of new;
She made forty gallons of black strap,
And forty gallons of wivvy wink,
And forty gallons of terrible drink,

and this must be some of the terrible drink.'

'Brewing is like a fat pig; it's all profit. You can sell everything, even to the skimmings,' proceeded the landlord.

'Teach me how to make it.' I replied.

'A bushel of malt and one pound of hops will make eighteen gallons of beer and nine gallons of ale; but if you want

SIMOND'S BREWERY, BRIDGE STREET, READING

body in it just do as I tell you. Boil your water for the mash and empty it into the tub, steeping the hops in a separate vessel. When the steam has gone off the tub, so that you can see your face in the water, and not before, put in your malt and stir it, then cover with a sack and leave it for nine hours, giving it a rout now and then. In the meantime, clean out your casks and have your cooling-tub ready. Draw off the sweet-wort, set the grains aside for the ale, put the liquor, with the hops, into the boiler, which must be iron or copper, and not zinc, and simmer for one hour. And now, if you want extra good beer, tap an old sycamore tree with an augur and get a quart of juice and mix it with the liquor; or get a bunch of carrots, parsnips, or beetroot, split them with a knife, and throw them into the boiler. At the end of an hour strain into the cooling-vat, saving the hops, and mix a dozen pounds of coarse brown sugar, or treacle, with the sweet-wort and put in the barm at blood-heat. The following morning take what barm you require, put it into strong bottles and bury it in the earth, where it will keep as long as you please; and remember that barm wants changing for seed, and that a tablespoonful of barm with a little brandy is the best thing in the world for a stoppage and has saved many a man's life. If you wish you can put it in the cask the same night; but it will be better to wait for twenty-four hours, at least. Well cork the barrel and fill to the bung-hole, saving a little to make up for each day's waste. Look at the barrel to see that it ferments. At the end of a fort-

OCK STREET MORRIS MEN, ABINGDON

THE BELL INN, SOUTH WESTALL

AMERSHAM

night take two handfuls of dry hops and put them into the barrel, stir with a stick and bung up. To make new beer appear old pour a little vinegar into the bung-hole; but to be good and strong it needs to be kept from six to twelve months; that is, from October till October comes again.'

Alfred Williams

A Near Thing

Two men, Chapman of Black Snail cottage and Charlie Gregory of Lockinge Kiln, were taking their reaping machines along a road near Ardington House when a donkey in a meadow came clumsily galloping and braying near Gregory's horses. They took fright and bolted, and Gregory saw that if he could not stop them they would run down Chapman for a certainty. On his right ran a strong iron fence, and he pulled the reins so that the reaping machine caught in the fence and was locked there. He was flung off and severely hurt, but his mate escaped untouched. He told me all about it when I visited him at his house beyond the Ridge Way, and how the thought of Chapman's 'long little family' rushed into his mind when he knew that the horses might be on the top of him, and that was

ROAD ACCIDENT, COOKHAM

why he pulled them into the iron railings. And then came one of the rare and precious confidences which countrymen will sometimes bestow on their clergy, 'Never do I put the horses into their work in the morning but I say "Lord send us right to-day".' The Lord did send him right when in that fraction of a second he thought not of himself but of his friend.

James Cornish

RURAL REVENGE

Below Day's Lock on the west bank is Little Wittenham Wood, one hundred acres of standard and coppice. The standard trees are good oaks and the coppice partly hazel and partly ash stools, an excellent wood for beauty and for sport. Between it and the river is a sloping meadow about which a story may be told.

One evening, Mr Latham, the tenant of the farm, who lived across the river at Dorchester, saw that a party of tourists had tied up their boat and pitched a tent in the meadow, so he asked them whether they had obtained leave to camp there.

No, they had not asked leave, and did not mean to do so, and were decidedly rude. Now Mr Latham was a County Councillor and expected to be treated as such; also he was not a safe man to attempt to play a rough game with; but on this occasion he was unusually quiet and rode away, saying very little. Next day, when he made his morning round, his 'Fogger', i.e. cowman, hailed him: 'Master, there was a rare to do in the wood meadow last night. I heerd folk a'hollering, and when I got down there was a lot of folk in a boat going on like anything, and the bull he was stamping on their tent and ripping it with his horns. I had a rare job to get him out of the meadow. I wonder who left the gate open?' 'Ah,' said Mr Latham, 'I do wonder who could have done that.'

James Cornish

THE VILLAGE CHRISTMAS

Christmas in those far-away days was very often a 'white' one – not always, snowy, but what was lovelier still, a sparkling hoar frost.

GATEKEEPER, COOKHAM DEAN

TWYFORD

About ten days before Christmas the excitement began. Every evening as we sat round the fire, with shutters bolted and curtains drawn, we children would wonder, 'Who will come tonight?' Then up the gravel outside the windows would come the slow tramp of heavy feet, and after a few minutes delay for whispered instructions, up would strike the village brass band. Instead of the usual 'Rule Britannia' or 'Two Little Girls in Blue', they would play the good old Christmas hymns, 'While shepherds watched' and 'Hark! the herald angels', etc. After a good long programme they would pause, hoping the door would open, and money be handed out – which, of course, always happened!

After evening the handbell ringers would come. I think I hear them now, the sweet tones of the bells ringing out on the frosty air.

Various small bands of children sang hymns and simple carols, hoping for money for Christmas fare. They were not disappointed; the spirit of generosity was abroad. But the real carol singers were men and women from the church and chapel choirs. They practised for weeks and although untrained, sang most beautifully, not in unison but all taking their separate parts. They would stand in a circle, with the light from their horn lanterns shining on their solemn rapt faces. The light was dim, being only from a home-made tallow candle, but they were used to dark nights and unlighted roads, and knew all the words by heart. Carol singing was their offering to the celebration of Christ's birthday. But to us children the high spot of Christmas entertainment was the visit of the mummers. About eight or nine men would arrive outside the house, and strike up:

> 'God bless the master of this house,
> We hope he is within.
> And if he is, pray tell us so
> And us'll soon step in.
> We hopes the mistress is within
> A-settin' by the fire,
> An' pitying us poor mummers, yer
> Out in the mud and mire.
> We don't come 'ere but once a year
> And hope 'tis no offence,
> But, if it is, pray tell us so
> And we will soon go hence.
> For we be come this Christmas time
> 'A purpose to be merry.'

My father would then open the door and invite them into our large paved kitchen, and the show would begin, watched with

NEWBURY

bated breath by all of us ten children, our parents, the maids, and any visitors there might be.

The mummers were led by Father Christmas in the correct attire, and long white beard. He stumped round, leaning on his stick, and reciting:

> 'Christmas comes but once a year
> And when it comes, it brings good cheer,
> Roast beef, plum pudden, mince pies.
> The geese are getting fat,
> Please to put a penny in the old man's hat.'

Then he would introduce 'King George' – a fine, upstanding young man (incidentally the village gamekeeper) resplendent in a navy-blue uniform and much yellow braid. He was asked to fight the 'Turk', who proved to be a man with a very black face and a very odd costume.

They immediately set to, and after much sword play and dodging round and round the ring, the 'Turk' falls to the ground, lying silent and still. Father Christmas then calls, 'Is there a doctor to be found?' and out steps a man in a long black coat and top hat. From his black bag he takes a bottle, and says, 'In this bottle I have medicine to cure the itch, the stitch, the palsy and the gout; pains within, and pains without. I drop a drop into the palm of the dead man's hand, and a drop on his tongue and say to him, "Turk, arise, and get thee back to thine own country"!'

The cure is instantaneous; the Turk arises and joins the rest of the company, who all add something to the play. I remem-ber one little fat man who always had a row of dolls of various sizes on his back. He says:

> 'In come I, little happy Jack,
> With my wife and family on my back.
> My head he's big, but my wits are small,
> So I brought my fiddle to please 'ee all.'

Then they all dance round until large jugs of beer appear, and a huge dish of mince pies – made specially for the occasion.

The theme of the play, no doubt, dates back to the Middle Ages, but it varied in every county.

In our village it carried on very successfully until the First World War. Now, I fear, all mummers are extinct.

Those were happy days! Everybody in the village contributed something to the spirit of Christmas, if only by collecting holly and ivy for decorating the church, where on Christmas morning men, women and children met to praise the new-born King and to wish each other the old, old wish, 'A Merry Christmas'.

Jane Taylor

ON THE ROAD

William Gordon Stables, retired naval Surgeon and Victorian eccentric, commissioned the building of the first caravan, The Wanderer, that was to be used solely for touring and holiday use. Known as the Gentleman Gypsy, he first took to the road in the early 1880s.

'THE WANDERER' CARAVAN

Early in May I left my village to enjoy a taste of gipsy life in earnest – a week on the road.

Matilda is a splendid mare, and a very handsome one. Strong and all though she be, there was in my mind a doubt as to whether she could drag the Wanderer on day after day at even the rate of ten miles in twenty-four hours.

It had been raining the night before, and as the road from our yard leads somewhat up hill, it was no wonder that, the immense caravan stuck fast before it got out of the gate. This was a bad beginning to a gipsy cruise, and, as a small concourse of neighbours had assembled to witness the start, was somewhat annoying. But a coal-carter's horse came to the rescue, and the start was finally effected.

Matilda took us through Twyford at a round trot, and would fain have broken into a gallop, but was restrained. But the long hill that leads up from the *Loddon Bridge* took the extra spirit out of her, and she soon settled down to steady work.

There is a pretty peep of Reading to be caught from the top of the railway bridge. No traveller should miss seeing it. Rested at Reading, our smart appearance exciting plenty of curiosity. It was inside that the crowd wanted to peep – it is inside all crowds want to peep, and they are never shy at doing so.

The town of Reading is too well known to need description; its abbey ruins are, however, the best part of it, to my way of thinking.

The day was as fine as day could be, the sky overcast with grey clouds that moderated the sun's heat.

Our chosen route lay past Calcot Park, with its splendid trees, its fine old solid-looking, red-brick mansion, and park of deer. This field of deer, I remember, broke loose one winter. It scattered in all directions; some of the poor creatures made for the town, and several were spiked on railings. The people had 'sport', as they called it, for a week.

It was almost gloomy under the trees that here overhang the road. Matilda was taken out to graze, the after-tent put up, and dinner cooked beneath the caravan. Cooked! ay, and eaten too with a relish one seldom finds with an indoor meal!

On now through Calcot village, a small and straggling little place, but the cottages are neat and pretty, and the gardens were all ablaze with spring flowers, and some of the gables and verandahs covered with flowering clematis.

The country soon got more open, the fields of every shade of green – a gladsome, smiling country, thoroughly English.

This day was thoroughly enjoyable, and the mare Matilda did her work well. Unhorsed and encamped for the night in the comfortable yard of the Crown Inn.

When one sleeps in his caravan in an inn yard one does not need to be called in the morning; far sooner than is desirable in most instances, dogs bark or rattle their chains, cows moan in their stalls, and horses clatter uneasily by way of expressing their readiness for breakfast. By-and-by ostlers come upon the scene, then one may as well get up as lie a-bed.

43

TWYFORD

Though all hands turned out at seven o'clock a.m., it was fully eleven before we got under way, for more than one individual was curious to inspect us, and learn all the outs and ins of this newest way of seeing the country. The forenoon was sunny and bright, and the roads good, with a coldish head-wind blowing.

Both road and country are level after leaving Theale, with plenty of wood and well-treed braelands on each side. This for several miles.

Jack's Booth, or the Three Kings, is a long, low house-of-call that stands by the wayside at cross roads: an unpleasant sort of place to look at. By the way, who was Jack, I wonder, and what three kings are referred to? The name is suggestive of card playing. But it may be historical.

The fields are very green and fresh, and the larks sing very joyfully, looking no bigger than midges against the little fleecy cloudlets.

I wonder if it be more difficult for a bird to sing on the wing than on a perch. The motion, I think, gives a delightful tremolo to the voice.

My cook, steward, valet, and general factotum is a lad from my own village, cleanly, active, and very willing, though not gifted with too good a memory, and apt to put things in the wrong places – my boots in the oven, for instance!

He sleeps on a cork mattress in the after-compartment of the Wanderer, and *does not snore*. A valet who snored would be an unbearable calamity in a caravan.

Hurricane Bob, my splendid Newfoundland, sleeps in the saloon on a morsel of red blanket. He does snore sometimes, but if told of it immediately places his chin over his fore-paw, and in this position sleeps soundly without any nasal sonance.

On our way to Woolhampton – our dining stage – we had many a peep at English rural life that no one ever sees from the windows of a railway carriage. Groups of labourers, male

THATCHAM

WILLIAM GORDON STABLES

and female, cease work among the mangolds, and, leaning on their hoes, gaze wonderingly at the Wanderer. Even those lazy workaday horses seem to take stock of us, switching their long tails as they do so in quite a businesslike way. Yonder are great stacks of old hay, and yonder a terribly-red brick farm-building, peeping up through a cloudland of wood.

We took Matilda out by the roadside at Woolhampton. This village is very picturesque; it lies in a hollow, and is surrounded by miniature mountains and greenwood. The foliage here is even more beautiful than that around Twyford.

We put up the after-tent, lit the stove, and prepared at once to cook dinner – an Irish stew, made of a rabbit, rent in piecs, and some bacon, with sliced potatoes – a kind of cock-a-leekie. We flavoured it with vinegar, sauce, salt, and pepper. It was an Irish stew – perhaps it was a good deal Irish, but it did not eat so very badly, nor did we dwell long over it. The fresh air and exercise give one a marvellous appetite, and we were hungry all day long.

But every one we met seemed to be hungry too. A hunk of bread and bacon or bread and cheese appears to be the standing dish. Tramps sitting by the wayside, navvies and road-men, hawkers with barrows – all were carving and eating their hunk.

A glorious afternoon.

With cushions and rugs, our broad dicky makes a most comfortable lounge, which I take advantage of. Here one can read, can muse, can dream, in a delightfully lethargic frame of

COOKHAM

mind. Who would be a dweller in dusty cities, I wonder, who can enjoy life like this?

Foley – my valet – went on ahead on the Ranelagh Club (our caravan tricycle) to spy out the land at Thatcham and look for quarters for the night.

There were certain objections to the inn he chose, however; so, having settled the Wanderer on the broad village green, I went to another inn.

A blackish-skinned, burly, broad-shouldered fellow answered my summons. Gruff he was in the extreme.

'I want stabling for the night for one horse, and also a bed for my driver.' This from me.

'Humph! I'll go and see,' was the reply.

'Very well; I'll wait.'

The fellow returned soon.

'Where be goin' to sleep yourse'f?'

This he asked in a tone of lazy insolence.

I told him mildly I had my travelling saloon caravan. I thought that by calling the Wanderer a saloon I would impress him with the fact that I was a gentleman-gypsy.

Here is the answer in full.

'Humph! Then your driver can sleep there too. We won't 'ave no wan (van) 'osses 'ere; and wot's more, we won't 'ave no wan folks!'

My Highland blood got up; for a moment I measured that man with my eye, but finally I burst into a merry laugh, as I

remembered that, after all, Matilda was only a 'wan' horse, and we were only 'wan' folks.

In half an hour more both Matilda and my driver were comfortably housed, and I was having tea in the caravan.

Thatcham is one of the quietest and quaintest old towns in Berkshire. Some of the houses are really studies in primeval architecture. I could not help fancying myself back in the Middle Ages. Even that gruff landlord looked as if he had stepped out of an old picture, and were indeed one of the beef-eating, bacon-chewing retainers of some ancient baronial hall.

It was somewhat noisy this afternoon on the village green. The young folks naturally took us for a show, and wondered what we did, and when we were going to do it.

Meanwhile they amused themselves as best they could. About fifty girls played at ball and 'give-and-take' on one side of the green, and about fifty boys played on the other.

The game the boys played was original and remarkable for its simplicity. Thus, two lads challenged each other to play, one to be deer, the other to be hound. Then round and round and up and down the green they sped till finally the breathless hound caught the breathless deer. Then 'a ring' of the other lads was formed, and deer and hound had first to wrestle and then to fight. And *wae victis*! the conquered lad had no sooner declared himself beaten than he was seized and thrown on his back, a rope was fastened to his legs, and he was drawn twice

ABINGDON SCHOOL REGATTA

ABINGDON SCHOOL REGATTA

round the ground by the juvenile shouting mob, and then the fun began afresh. A game like this is not good for boys' jackets, and tailors must thrive in Thatcham.

William Gordon Stables MD RN

THE REGATTA

We are glad to be able to report a marked improvement in the affairs of the Boating Club, the powers that be having at last put away the spirit of inaction which was prevailed for the last few years. Following on the races, which we gave accounts of in our last number we have to publish particulars of a Regatta held at the end of last term. A suggestion to hold such a Regatta was eagerly caught up, and in a meeting convened for the purpose a committee was chosen representing past and present boys. The day fixed for the races was Wednesday, July 28th, which turned out a fine day and a large number of the friends of the boys assembled to witness the racing. A stern official supplied by the Thames Conservancy kept the course clear and all arrangements were perfect. The Head Master kindly officiated as judge; J.T. Morland, Esq., was umpire; and L.W. Paul, Esq., starter.

ABINGDON MILL

The principal event of the afternoon was the annual race between crews of past and present Abingdonians.

The crews were made up as follows:

Present.	Past.
bow. P.H. Morland	bow. F.H. Pryce
2. H. Anwyl	2. F.J. Robinson
3. W.L. Russwurm	3. W.E. Robinson
str. W.T. Morland	str. R. Shopland
cox. P.A. Holmes	cox. A.B. Morland

The past crew were rather the more powerful of the two but were of course in very inferior training. However they got off well and extending themselves to their utmost managed to keep the lead till about fifty yards from the winning post. Here one of their crew had the misfortune to catch a fine healthy 'crab' and the others also thoroughly collapsing, the school crew gradually came up to them and finally won a close and exciting race by about half a length. The winners thoroughly deserved their victory as they had trained hard in the term and rowed very pluckily when they seemed to be having the worst of the race; they were warmly cheered at the finish. For the past W.E. Robinson rowed splendidly and was the only one who was able to last the course.

The Abingdonian [Abingdon School Magazine] 1892

ABINGDON FAIR

Perhaps an apology is needed for the subject I have chosen, and an apology I am quite prepared to make. Two subjects were proposed to me, one was the history of the School, and the other that of the Fifth Form. Both of these I had to decline, but for different reasons; of the first I know, I am ashamed to say, too little, of the second too much, and though I have often threatened to publish some of the work produced by the present Fifth, with a correct translation annexed for the benefit of past Fifth Forms, I thought it best to postpone my intention till a time when the present Fifth can look with a smile on the strange vagaries of to-day. For these reasons I was unable to fall in with either of the suggestions made to me; and left to my own resources after passing in review and rejecting many ideas that suggested themselves to me, I fixed my choice at last on this, 'A Village Fair'; my reason being that it was in the events of the term; for all knew Abingdon Fair.

A fair, or rather to give it its proper name, a Feast, is the great event of the village year, the one general holiday to take part in which all the absent members of a family are expected to return. In a town of any importance they have adopted a new and more imposing term, the old feast has become gala, and a parachute descent and other attractions are added; but as a rule the people are left to their own resources for amusement; for with the exception of a few rifle galleries, a stall or two, and the inevitable coconuts, there is but little assistance

ABINGDON

from without. One man however had found it possible to strike out a new line even in the show business; he appeared at a small window and invited people to shy at him; one shot a penny; in case he was hit, a thing which was of very rare occurrence he got his revenge by giving a cigar to the successful thrower; even an agricultural labourer cannot smoke everything. The festival begins on Saturday and lasts over Monday. The principal events are two cricket matches, a home match on Saturday for the purpose of selecting a team for the great game with some neighbouring village on Monday, then sports, and the proceedings are wound up by a dance. The foreign match is often played for a dinner, and then there is great scope for the umpire. The LBW rule comes in very useful to the side which looks like losing. In the match that I witnessed, the visitors were having the worst of the game, when their best man was given out leg before. Then the row began; the batsman refused to go and was backed up by the rest of his team, who appealed to their umpire. He gave it as his opinion that a man could not be out unless he knowingly and wilfully put his leg in front of his wicket; and this he was sure that his man had not done. The visitors' captain objected to the umpire, and produced a copy of the rules, a careful study of which had brought him to the conclusion, that if he objected to the Umpire, the decision on account of which objection was taken, was thereby invalidated. The discussion seemed

likely to end in a general fight, but the visitors seeing that they would have in all probability to fight the crowd as well, wisely gave in, and the match proceeded. The interval however was very near fatal to the home team; for their umpire, the village drunkard, had made good use of the opportunity, and had forgotten which way he was playing; and his next decision gave the opposite side so much pleasure that they plied him with refreshments so generously, that he was soon gloriously drunk, and gave both sides out indiscriminately; and it was only the advantage that the home team had gained at the beginning of the game that enabled them to win the match.

After the cricket match came the sports. They began with a horse race for bridles. Then there was a waltzing competition, in which the competitors displayed, if little grace, at any rate much vigour; the principles on which the judges made their award, are probably known to the judges alone. After that there was a treacle loaf eating contest, confined to boys. A platform was erected on which the competitors were stationed with their hands bound behind their backs, and from a bar above great lumps of bread, soaked in treacle, were suspended by strings, in such a way that each lump was on a level with a boy's mouth. At this bait they rose like fishes for some time; but, at last, one cleverer than the rest, caught his in his mouth, and pushed it against his neighbour's back, and holding it firmly with his nose, proceeded to devour it amidst the cheers

49

ABINGDON

of the spectators. Then followed a smoking contest; about two dozen men got into a waggon and were provided with long churchwardens, which were carefully inspected by the umpire after they had been filled, to see that everything was fair. The competitors were told that they should present themselves, together with the ashes, as they were finished. On the signal being given there was a frantic striking of matches; for there was a fairly strong wind blowing, and it was by no means easy in their exposed position to get a light; then most of the competitors puffed away till they were about black in the face; but one wily rustic blew down his pipe and finished before the others were well begun, and marched off triumphantly to the umpire, but came back surprized and indignant; he had been asked to produce the ashes. He evidently wished to address the people on the subject of his wrongs, but soon gave up the attempt, for his complaint only called forth jeers and laughter. In the egg and spoon race I noticed another cute rustic, who, having got his egg, carefully let it fall and then smeared his spoon with the contents, hoping, that if he could procure a fresh egg, in doing which he met with little difficulty, the broken egg would hold the other fast. In the race, however, he found that his theory could not stand the test of practice.

The day ended with a dance in the village schoolroom, a dance, which, owing to the limited space was very select, those who were not considered respectable enough, of course gave out that they never had any intention of being present;

married people with the exception of two or three matrons to act as chaperons to the whole company, were also excluded. The floor was waxed by cutting up a wax candle into minute pieces, but the nails which stood out here and there above the well-worn boards were left untouched, and I heard the Master of the Ceremonies congratulating his partner, that, in the course of the first dance he had only hit upon one. The music was provided by a couple of fiddlers who went on playing till the MC gave them a whistle to show that he had had enough. As to the costumes, one of the guests had a dress suit and another a frock coat, whilst a third, an agricultural labourer, had a pair of white kid gloves, which he seemed to regard with mingled feelings, pride when he was asking for a dance, shame when some of his friends called public attention to them.

One spectator there, was the village prophet. Standing apart from the crowd and looking with pity not unmingled with contempt on the giddy multitude, as he was accustomed to style the people, when he took up his parable against them on the Sunday after the feast in the Wesleyan chapel, of which he was a great upholder. Such was his appearance in public, but in private his wife used to speak to him as a silly auld man; for the money which he had saved by starving his family, he had lent and lost.

The Abingdonian [Abingdon School Magazine] 1890

MORLANDS BREWERY, ABINGDON

IN PRAISE OF ABINGDON ALE

When I go down to Boar's Hill,
That's hard by Oxford town,
I drink the song of nightingales,
I drink – and who shall frown –
The ale they brew in Oxfordshire
That hummeth bright and brown.

When I go down to Boar's Hill,
That's over Hinksey vale,
I drink the smell of gorse and pine,
I drink – and who shall rail –
The ale they brew in Abingdon
That is a noble ale.

When I go down to Boar's Hill,
Where noted bards reside,
I drink great draughts of taintless air,
I drink – and who shall chide –
Great draughts of ale in little inns,
And let the poets bide.

C.H.B. (The Berkshire Book)

THE BAKED BRITCHES

William Breakspear, the sturdy old carter of Woolstone, with corduroy suit, billycock hat, and leather gaiters reaching above the knees, stumped into the stable carrying a chalk-soiled overcoat under his arm, with broad flag-basket and brass-handled whip in the hand, which he first of all deposited on top of the big wooden corn-bin, and then proceeded to harness black 'Diamond,' who stood grinding her food in the manger and blowing out her nose now and then, making the chaff fly. He pushed the big collar over her eyes and ears – she thrusting her head forward to assist the operation – turned it right side up, clapped on the hames, fitted the blind halter, pad, and breaching tackle, and buckled up the belly-band, with a snatch of song that old Farmer Brooks, of Stanford-in-the-Vale, used to sing every year at harvest-home:

A sack o' wild oats in our youthful days,
And we're happier when they're gone.

Then he turned the mare's head round to the door, and addressed the youngster in the next stall:

'Come an, ther, an' fetch thaay two along to tha drill. We be gwain to put thaay black cyarter's wuts in to-daay. Breng thi

BURGHFIELD

cwut along wi tha. I warn thee't want un a dinner-time. 'Tis a main percin' blaw ayant tha owl' White 'Oss tha smarnin'. We could do wi tha owl' shepherd's leather britches very well.'

'What sart o' britches be thaay, then?' the youth inquires, with a grin.

'Why, essent a never yerd tell o' owl' Joby Cark an' 'is leather britches? A got 'em wet-droo, an' tha missis put 'em in tha o-ven to dry, thas know'st, an' a couldn't get 'em an tha nex' marnin'. Zo a started blerin' a bit. Then tha owl' dooman begun an to 'n. "Thee must thenk o' thi namesake, dost know, Job, an' hae patience, like 'e did." "Aa, begad mun,' Job zed," "but 'e was never fooast to wer baked britches, like I got to." Jest put thi nammet down, an' 'elp I wi that owl' graay a minute, oot. Now then, ther, stan' awver. Tha bist too fat to mauve. Tha oostn't draa a sprat off a gridiron. Tha's moore at it! Now we be awright. Gee up, ther!' And off they go singing:

> Tha owl' black 'oss is no longer in tha stall,
> Drat tha owl' 'oss! I'm jolly glad a's gone;
> For a oodn't do na work, an' a was no good at all;
> Drat tha owl' 'oss! I'm jolly glad a's gone.
> Hi-i-o,
> Tha stall in tha stable's empty;
> Hi-i-o,
> For tha owl' black 'oss is gone.

Alfred Williams

A TALE OF WEST HENDRED

The Duck House was a little low mud-built cottage, some two hundred years old, consisting of a kitchen, a bedroom raised one step above the former and a tiny cupboard dignified by the style and title of 'pant'ny'. The hut owed its name to its proximity to the brook, and to the fact that during a more than usually rainy season it was apt to be flooded. On these occasions the water would come lappering over the stones of the court, and without so much as 'by your leave' would make its way into the kitchen, where it rioted at will, to the exceeding inconvenience of the legitimate inmates.

Old Shadrach and Sarah, whose home it had been for the last forty years, were of opinion that no cottage in the village could compare with it. Beneath its thatched roof they had begun married life; and sons had been born to them there, who were stalwart men now and had long since made for themselves new homes across the sea. In the squatter's hut, to which the old people clung with the affection conceived of association, they aspired to end their days – a modest ambition, the sole survivor of those with which they had set out on life's journey together. The hope of recent years was the acquisition of the Duck House. To this end they had scraped and toiled, denying themselves all save the barest necessaries, working early and late to add a shilling here, a sixpence there, until at length the requisite sum was almost complete.

When things went awry, and the master's temper was more than usually 'ock'erd'; when Shadrach's rheumatism was

SULHAM FARM WORKERS

LUDBRIDGE MILL, EAST HENDRED

troublesome, or Sarah felt 'that low an' queer'; when in short the aged couple were sensible of the need of a mental stimulant, the door would be locked, the blind closely drawn, and the stocking brought forth from its hiding place. Its contents would be poured into Sarah's lap, and the two would count up their hoard – nearly ten pounds in solid money. Half-crowns, shillings, sixpences, threepenny-bits, piles of pennies – each one meaning a pipe foregone on Shadrach's part – coins of every description were represented, from the lowly farthing to the rare sovereign gleaming among baser metal.

'Lawk-a-mussy-me!' exclaimed the old man one evening, as he sat watching his wife's fingers lose themselves in the mass, 'I dwunno, Sally, howsumdiver I shall bring myself to part wi' 't: 'twull be like tearin' the heart out o' my body. Dear, dear, wot a pity as a thing cassn't be boughten wi'out bein' paid fur!'

'That's as true a word as iver you said in your life. I shall miss the brass sore, an' 'twull be ter'ble unked when there be nothen to screw an' scruple fur. We've got but two days moor to look at he an' count 'un ovver, now that he o'ny wants eighteen-pence of the ten pound. If you gi'es ma that a-Friday when you tek's your wages, it can all be paid to Muster Huggins a-Saturday, which 'ull save we this wik's rent, seein' as how he couldn't ha' the meanness to ax we fur that, when we ha' just paid 'un sich a comenjous lot down!'

'Aye, aye,' returned the other, adding regretfully, 'Pon my sowl I'd as lief get rid o' the 'en as the money; I 'udn't miss she sa much.'

'But *I* should; an' I'd let 'ee knaw that 'tis my 'en, an' not to be got rid on, or giv' away fur brass. She be a livin' cratur', an' this year be o'ny filthy lucre, as parson sez; though why a calls it 'filthy' I dwunno, 'cause most on it be clane anuff. But that's neether year nor ther'. My 'en, wot lays sa reg'lar ben't a-gwine to be—'

'Ther' be no call fur 'ee to snap my yead off; narra one wasn't thinkin' o' interferin' wi' she.

'No, they'd best not,' was Sarah's significant reply, which her husband received in respectful silence.

The subject of this dispute had been presented as a chicken to the old woman. It had now developed into 'a strutty little hen,' and repaid its mistress's care by a conscientious discharge of its duty in the matter of eggs. Sarah's affection for her solitary chick gave the neighbours at first much food for merriment.

On the morning of the fateful day – for such indeed it proved to be – that was to see the coping-stone placed on the labour of years, Shadrach went forth to work as usual. He was employed in 'bird-starving' on a strip of land some distance from the village and contiguous to the highway. It was a dull chilly occupation, this walking round a field to occasionally

VACHEL ALMSHOUSES, READING

fire a rusty gun at invisible rooks, and it must be confessed that he devoted a disproportionate amount of attention to that part of his beat which bordered on the road, where there was a possibility of exchanging the 'time o' day' with passing travellers. He was a simple-minded, sociable individual, and was quite ready for the sake of a chat, to offer a share of his frugal lunch to a tramp who accosted him, as he sat on the bank skirting the Turnpike.

'Have 'ee got a copper fur a chap as ha'n't tasted a mossel o' food to-day gaffer?'

Shadrach replied in all sincerity that he had not 'a brass farden' about him.

'I might ha' knowed that by the look on you,' said the tramp, and he also took a seat on the bank.

'How fur's the nearest public, an' wot kind o' lan'lerd kips it – one as 'ud give a drink to a poor feller who's dyin' o' thirst?'

'Ah, that be wusser nor hunger,' remarked the old man sympathetically. 'I'd ha' gin' 'ee a penny an' welcome, but my ole ooman kips ma rayther shart'

'Gar-on,' was the tramp's impolite rejoinder. 'I've heard that tale afore.'

'D'ee think I'd tell 'ee a lie? As sure as I sets year I gi'es she ivery penny I yarns, an' what's left ovver from rent an' fire an' vittles, she puts in the stockin' under the mattress.'

'You've got a stockin' wi' mebbe a couple o' pounds in't?'

'Couple! We've ten pound, shart by eighteen-pence which as how I manes to put in to-night from my wages. That be God's truth!'

The other whistled and turned away his head to hide the greedy light in his eyes. 'Wi' all that sight o' money you wun't sper' a ha'p'ny to a chap as ha'n't tasted a mossel o' food these two days – 'tis 'ard, crool 'ard!'

Shadrach's heart melted within him. 'Year, tek' my nunchin',' he said; 'or if thee've a mindt to goo into yon village, I meks no doubt but what my missus 'ull gi'e 'ee a drap o' tay an' a crust o' bread.'

'I'd walk twice as fur to get summat to eat. What's your name, an' whereabouts do you live?'

'We lives in the Duck House close alongside the water; arra-one 'ull tell 'ee wher' to find 'un—'

'Thank 'ee gaffer, thank 'ee kindly; may God blesh you!' and the tramp swung oft towards the village at an astonishing pace considering his state of starvation.

When the old fellow returned from work that evening, his wife informed him that she had 'bin a'most frowtened to death by a girt travellin' man as come an' axed fur food: said some 'un had told 'un that the lady wot lived in the Duck House niver turned arra-one from her door wi'out a mossel o'

55

CHARNEY BASSETT

bread. Wher' a got that lie I dwunno, but I wur fust to gi'e 'un summat, 'cause he med ha' took all as he fancied, an' wi' them ten pound lyin' betwixt the mattress and the bed-boord, I 'udn't ha' aggreevated 'un not fur wotiver.'

An idea flashed into Shadrach's mind – an idea so horrible that for a moment his head swam, and he clutched at the table to save himself from falling.

'A didn't steal nothen', I s'pwose?' he asked in a voice he scarce recognized as his own.

Happily Sarah failed to observe his emotion, being engaged in preparing supper.

'No, a went off as quiet as a lamb, bless 'ee. He found the 'en right away up the road, an' come back to tell ma on't – you can think as I cut an' run arter she when I yeard that. 'Twur a comacal thing she should ha' strayed sa fur; I niver knawed she do't afoor.'

Shadrach breathed again. 'Now then, missus,' he said when the meal was ended and his pipe well alight, 'fetch out the brass, an' we 'ull gi'e 'un a last count ovver – yer be the eighteenpence.'

Sarah disappeared for a few seconds into the bedroom, to return with a vast knitted stocking tied round the top by a piece of string.

'Sims wunnerful heavy,' she remarked.

'An' I dwun't sim to year the chinkle-chankle,' added her husband.

It was opened, and the contents were poured into her lap, but as they came to light a cry of wrath and anguish broke from the pair.

'The money! Wher' be the money? Oh, Lor' if it be stole!'

They turned the stocking inside out; they rushed to the bed and searched it from end to end, shaking the pillows and blankets and pounding the mattress in vain. They turned the house topsy-turvy, leaving no cranny unexplored, but the hard truth was not to be shirked, that the savings of years were gone and that a number of pebbles had been substituted in their place.

''Tis that tramp as stealed it,' moaned Sarah, rocking herself backwards and forwards; 'to think that a drap o' tea an' a crust o' bread should ha' cost ma sa dear! Oh my, oh my!'

Shadrach said nothing, but he thought a great deal.

TWYFORD FLOWER SHOW

'I kin see't plain anuff now,' continued the old woman; 'the 'en was peckin' about in the court when he come to the door; he just picked she up an' car'd she away, a-purpose to bamboodgel ma up the road.'

'Did you goo off an' leave 'un yer?' inquired her husband.

'I thought he wur comin' along behind ma – no, I wun't tell 'ee a lie. I just niver thought o' nothen 'cept the 'en. D'reckly my back was turned he must ha' slipped in an' teken the money.'

'I wunners if Hannah sin 'un pass her window,' mused Shadrach.

'Lard love 'ee, he 'udn't be that soft: he'd creep round the side o' the house an' acrass the fields – I reemembers now, thinkin' 'twur comacal I didn't meet 'un as I come back.'

'No doubt but what that be how he done't,' acquiesced the other, who seemed too crushed to make any moan.

'What I'd like to find out is this: how did a knaw as the brass wur ther'? I ha'n't breathed it to a livin' sowl. Ha' you, Shadrach Toomer?'

The suddenness of the question deprived him for a moment of speech: when, after a pause, he found his voice, he affirmed in accents of the deepest solemnity that never had the word money passed his lips.

Perhaps he did protest too much; perhaps his uneasy conscience betrayed itself in look or bearing. Certain it is that his wife glanced suspiciously at him once or twice before she deigned to accept his denial.

Evening after evening the aged pair sat one each side of the fire, Sarah expatiating on their trouble, for the poor old soul missed the money with an aching sense of loss, Shadrach

UPTON

57

TWYFORD FLOWER SHOW

endeavouring by a sedulous study of the Bible, to close his ears to her complaints. For a while she bore with this inattention. One night however, her patience gave way.

It was November, and the domestic atmosphere within was scarcely less gloomy than that without. Rain had been falling since dawn and at noon Shadrach had come home wet to the skin, complaining of rheumatic pains in 'the spine of his back.'

When, after supper, he fixed his glasses on his nose and opened the Book as usual, Sarah's irritation could no longer be subdued.

'Lark, what a lively 'un you are to live wi', to be sure! Set ther', 'ee 'ull, an' groan fit to bust your weskit, but niver a word do 'ee spake, bad nor good. Rade summat out o' the Bible, cassn't 'ee? It wun't do we no harm, an' 'ull help to pass the time along.'

He obeyed, choosing as his subject the history of the Flood, to which the dreary splash of the rain on the casement and the rush of the swollen stream added a touch of realism.

'Tis a wunner as Noah wurn't druv' silly wi' all they beasts,' he said as he closed the Book.

'I wishes as the Lard could ha' sin His way to drowndin' a few o' they naesty creepin' things: we 'udn't ha' missed them stingy waspes, an' we could ha' done wi'out blackbeetles, an' a few moor o' the same sort. Lor,' what a time Noah an' his fam'bly must ha' had, wi' all them swarmin', as you med say, in his house!

'I reckon us 'ull knaw summat about a flood presen'ly, if the bruk kips on a-risin', said Shadrach.

The loss of the money was for the moment forgotten in this fresh anxiety. His first thought next morning was of the stream; as soon as he was dressed he dragged himself with difficulty to the door – his rheumatism being now acute – and peered through the grey dawn at the rushing yellow torrent a few yards from him.

'Still risin', an' the rain comin' down fit to cut a haystack a-two,' he murmured.

The morning dragged slowly away. When Sarah had finished her household tasks, she sat fondly watching her hen as with gentle cluck-clucks, it pecked up the crumbs about the kitchen. Ere long the old woman's head dropped, and following her husband's example, she sank into a doze. They both were awakened by a loud cackle, indicating extraordinary agitation on the part of their pet. 'What a fuss about a hegg,' said the mistress drowsily, and was composing herself for a second

SHINFIELD

nap when Shadrach perceived the real cause of the commotion.

'Look alive missus! the water's runnin' unner the sill an' her nest be soppin' wet; she must lay her hegg by the fire.'

Sarah seized a broom, and opening the door, tried to brush out the intrusive element, thereby making matters worse, for now that the barrier was removed, the water rushed in like a miniature torrent. 'What be we do?' she cried in despair, 'as fasts as I hucks 'un out, he runs in agen!'

'Us must shut to the dooer an' bide till 'un sinks,' was his reply.

This, however, the water did not appear to have the least intention of doing. Gradually the pool in the middle of the floor spread until it reached the fire which, after a brief struggle, it vanquished amid spluttering and hissing.

'An' narra tater cooked fur dinner!' sobbed the old woman as she and her husband retreated to the upper end of the kitchen. Their stay here was brief; again they were forced to retire, and they finally took up their position on the bed, from which they could hear the relentless foe surging round their household goods, washing against the 'sofy' of which Sarah was so proud, straining at the dresser adorned with the best tea-set and the pictures of the two absent sons, curling about

the Windsor chairs that shone until you could almost see your face in them.

Presently there came a blast of cold air, and Shadrach, looking from the inner room, saw that the weight of water had burst open the outer door, and that the flood in the kitchen was rising by leaps and bounds. Many thoughts were working in his mind as he sat through the afternoon, which was long and yet cruelly short, till evening stole down while the stream creeping over the step mounted ever higher and higher.

'Missus,' began Shadrach when the last ray of light had faded, and they crouched side by side in the chill darkness, 'I cassn't get out i' this, along o' my pooer back; but ther' yen't no call fur you to be drownded. It dwun't sim a-sif arra-one be comin' to help we, so you had best try an' scamble through the water afoor 'tis too late.'

'Wher' you bides, I bides: we've lived ovver farty 'ear tergither, an' I ben't a-gwine to lave 'ee now. I've bin errible wi 'ee lately, Shade, but 'twur along o' that money, an' I axes your pardon, seein' as how you took it sa uncommon sweet.'

Shadrach's hand sought hers: 'Sally, ole ooman, promise as you'll furgimma fur what I be gwine to tell 'ee, an' that you wun't niver cast it up agin ma, if sa be as we gits through this year.'

59

HORN STREET, READING

GRIFFIN INN, READING

The pledge was given, and he proceeded to relate his encounter with the tramp: how, in the fullness of his pride, he had boasted of his wealth, even to describing where it was hidden; and had lied to his wife, allowing her to take upon herself the sole blame.

Sarah remained long silent. When she spoke it was to say – 'Pooer Shade, you meant no harm; but I *be* glad it wurn't the 'en arter all. Do 'ee knaw wher' she be?'

'No, I ha'n't sin she sence we come in year: I yeard a kind of a squawk a while back, an' it simmed a-sif she flod some'ers, o'ny I couldn't tell 'ee wher'.'

Again silence, broken this time by Shadrach: 'Missis, you be a good ooman – I niver knawed how good till now – but I'd feel moor comfer'ble-like in my mindt, if you'd upset ma a bit ovver that tramp job. It dwun't sim nat'ral fur 'ee to tek it sa quiet.'

'Not now, Shade; I couldn't upset 'ee now, when mebbe afoor many minutes is passed, we two 'ull be drowndin' like rats in a hole. Money dwun't sim o' much account when you looks at it wi' death stan'in' at your elber. Oh, to think as we should be cast away' – she broke into a wail – 'cast away to die in our strength, wi' our senses about us, to die *alive*, as you med say, on the bed wher' the li'le 'uns wur barned!'

'I didn't think we should ha' bin furgot by iverybody,' responded Shadrach plaintively.

The words had not left his lips, before a sickly yellow gleam shone on the water; a man's voice cried: 'Hello! wher' be?' and a few seconds later a young labourer, lantern in hand, splashed his way to the bedside.

'Ben't much too soon, simly,' was his laconic remark, as he held the light above his head and surveyed the scene: 'us had to see to the pigs and the fowls (lots of 'um be drownded), or we should ha' bin year afoor. Now then, which on you be comin' fust?'

'SPECIAL POULTRY CLASS', UNIVERSITY COLLEGE, READING

The two old people were carried through the house and up the court to the lane, where a farm cart was in readiness to convey them to a neighbour's house on higher ground.

Sarah's distress was acute at leaving without her hen, and the following morning she repaired betimes to the Duck-House. The flood had fallen considerably during the night, but there was still more water in the kitchen than was agreeable. And what a scene of desolation the whole of the interior presented! The floor and the furniture were 'smuddered' in mud, as she plaintively said; the 'sofy' was a sponge; the best table-cloth a dripping rag; worst of all, the children's 'picturs' were ruinated – 'it was anuff to gin arra-one a turn as 'ud last 'un the rest 'o your life.' At one sight, however, Sarah's heart leaped up, her troubles grew small: on the mantel-board, serene and placid, sat the hen, and when with a welcoming cry she alighted on her mistress's shoulder, a shining white egg was revealed to view upon the shelf.

During the next few days the owner of the Duck-House declared his intention of pulling the old place down, it being no longer fit for habitation. What caused him to change his mind people never rightly knew: the fact remained, that when the water had subsided, the old folks returned to their nest, and lived there in great peace and comfort until their death some years later. The gossips exhausted themselves in surmises

as to how the means for this state of things were supplied, and having turned Shadrach's and Sarah's affairs inside out, they came to the conclusion (which happened to be the correct one) that the two sons in Australia had sent their parents a considerable sum of money. The investigators were helped to this explanation by the knowledge – elicited through diligent enquiry at the post office – that a day or two after 'the girt flood, a queerish-lookin' letter from furrin parts' had been delivered at Sarah's door. It was further whispered that Shade had 'boughten the cottage ter'ble cheeup,' for he was heard more than once to remark that 'what you thinks is misfartin' yen't allus one; an' though the flood ruinated a smart deal o' the furnitoor an' midee'd the mattress, it sp'iled the ole 'ouse fur arra-one 'cept we; an' it larned ma what a good missus I'd got.' Which last observation, unmarried men said, was plainly absurd, because if he had not had time during forty years to discover what Sarah was, it was certain that sitting together an hour or two on a soppy bedstead would not teach him. The married men however, maintained a discreet silence: they knew that not even after forty years of wedded life would any-one, save a fool, presume to assert that he had fathomed the mysteries of one female mind.

Eleanor Hayden

WINDSOR CASTLE

Victoria At Windsor

Often, while at Windsor, she begins the day by a drive in her donkey chair, through the beautiful Home Park to Frogmore, where she breakfasts in the open air or in a tent, enjoying the freshness of the morning, and the sweetness of the woods and the lawns; though there is rarely absent a significant despatch box, containing what is the Queen's daily work, that continual supply of State papers which, important as they may be, are far from being light reading. 'After this little preface of the open air, which she always loves, her Majesty returns to a close morning's work with her Secretaries, when all important public business is gone over. Before the hour of luncheon she goes out again to take a drive. The luncheon midday meal is the most cheerful, the most expansive moment of the day, when the Queen is surrounded chiefly by her own children, and family matters are the principal subject of discussion and consultation. So abundant a family has, no doubt, many difficulties, as it has also many pleasant things to be talked over. In all that has been made visible to the public of the Queen's private diary and papers, and in the published letters of the Princess Alice, the crowd of Christian names (sometimes meaning the highest personages in Europe) is quite amusing. They seem to throng upon each other till the spectator can scarcely see through the crowd to the pleasant group at table, all telling the

QUEEN VICTORIA AT FROGMORE

HIGH STREET, WINDSOR

latest news of these friends and relatives, speculating what they will do next, laughing at a characteristic trait of this majesty or that. The same thing occurs, no doubt, in every large family; but few families are so large, or have so many largely extending ties, as that of the Queen.

Mrs Oliphant

THE QUEEN'S JOURNAL

Windsor Castle, December 2 1887

The Maharani and Gaikwar arrived in different carriages. At three I received her with Beatrice in the Audience-room. All the men were kept out of the way and the Indian attendants in particular. Lady Cross and Lady Waterpark brought the Maharani in, as well as her sister and Mrs Elliott, the wife of the gentleman who has been for long with the Gaikwar. The Maharani bent low and shook hands. She is a pretty little

thing, and wore a close-fitting jacket and trousers, no petticoat, of pale blue satin, over the whole a long crimson and gold gauze veil, which passed over the head, and covered her completely, excepting her face, which she uncovered as she came into the room. She had splendid jewels on. She looks very gentle, but is said to be very wilful, and to wish to see everything without being seen. She regretted not having seen Bertie. Both Princesses had a red spot painted in the centre of their foreheads. The Maharani understands a little English, and says a few words, but her sister does not. I ventured upon a sentence in Hindustani which Abdul and Mohamed had helped to teach me. I also presented Beatrice in Hindustani. The Maharani said she wished to see the Castle and, after she had sat a little while on the sofa next to me, she shook hands and took leave.

Then I received the Gaikwar of Baroda, accompanied by Lord Cross and Sir G. Fitzgerald. The Gaikwar is small, dark, and not distinguished or good-looking, but he seems very intelligent. He was dressed in white, and wore a low red tur-

63

QUEEN VICTORIA DINING AT WINDSOR CASTLE

THE GRANDSTAND, ASCOT

ban, or rather cap, and a necklace of large emeralds. He speaks English perfectly well.

December 8th

Saw the Duke of Norfolk, who is going to Rome to congratulate the Pope on my part on the fiftieth anniversary of his becoming Priest, and is bearer of an official as well as an autograph letter from me. The Duke spoke of his excellent uncle Lord Lyons' death, which occurred without his ever recovering consciousness. He is to be buried tomorrow at Arundel. Signed a great many papers. At seven, Lord Salisbury brought Count Corti to present his letters of recall, he having been summarily recalled. After this I saw Lord Salisbury, and spoke of the great success of the Unionist meeting in Dublin, a very large one, where Lord Hartington and Mr Goschen were enthusiastically received. This had given the Loyalists courage, and had done great good. There had been also another great and successful meeting in London. Lord Salisbury thinks the Government much stronger, and that there should be no moves or changes, in which I entirely agreed, as I said it unsettled everyone.

Queen Victoria

SPORT IN PARSON'S FIELD

The village was left to take care of itself while young and old, every soul the place could number, save the absolutely bedrid-

den, repaired to the parson's meadow, there to speed the sunny hours with the strains of a real brass band – no mere dulcimer and concertina – and sports many and curious, including a greasy pole surmounted by a leg of mutton. This last, if the truth be told, proved an occasion of blaspheming to more than one ambitious youth, the language that was expended on spoilt clothes and sore palms falling far short of a parliamentary standard. The prize was secured by a persevering lad, who, after repeated attempts, succeeded in attaining the goal of his desires, whence he descended with a rapidity that was involuntary on his part, to declare that he 'udn't niver goo up an' – emphatic – 'gr'asy pole agen, no, not if a whole sheep wur stuck a-top on', let alone a bally leg o' mutton!' a sentiment which his discomfited rivals heartily applauded. Over the men's tug-of-war (married versus single) excitement ran high, the matrons and the maids urging on with shrill cries their respective champions to the contest which took place across the brook. The struggle had swayed doubtfully backwards and forwards some minutes, when a sharp-eyed advocate of matrimonial bliss discovered that her side was short of its full complement by one, and proclaimed the fact with such insistence that proceedings were stayed while a brief consultation among the married team ensued as to whom should be chosen to fill the gap. A wag suggesting that the thatcher was a 'likely man, who did oughter pull fine seein' he've just took his second missus,' shouts were raised for 'Giley! wher' be our Giley then?'

DONNINGTON CASTLE, NEWBURY

Slowly the ponderous form of the thatcher heaved into view, striking dismay into his opponents, who had only just managed to hold their own before, and who shivered in anticipation of the wetting this doughty recruit seemed to promise them. With becoming solemnity he divested himself of his coat and waistcoat, handed them to Leah who exhorted him to 'goo on an' mind as he pulled they young chaps into the bruk,' and tightening his belt, took his place on the rope, a modest yet confident smile illuminating his weather-beaten visage, as who should say: 'Though "the battle is not always to the strong" the odds that we shall win this one are great.' And win it they did. From the moment the rope was drawn taut the Benedicks ran away with the bachelors, who suffered themselves to be dragged across the stream after a fashion which the girls stigmatized as 'summat ridic'lous and crool to see; the girt lot o' young safts!' at the same time giving their dripping swains to understand that the latter 'needn't think as we be gwine to let them objec's come anighst our best frocks, 'cause we ain't!'

Such heartless want of sympathy in their downfall occasioned some murmuring among the single men, who were thereupon counselled by the matrons to 'goo an' get wed as soon as you can find an ooman to tek you; a man be never no good till he's married (not over much then, neether!) an' all you young chaps 'ud be twicet what you be now, if you'd each a missus to look arter 'ee.'

It was useless to combat these opinions, supported as they were by the husbands' superior bulk; the insulted youths could only receive them in silence, and resolve to remedy the defect as speedily as might be.

Of all the events that day the married women's race was the most mirth-provoking. The prize – a long length of white calico – was earnestly coveted by mothers of families, and was responsible for the large number of entries. A stranger lot of competitors surely never awaited the starter's signal! Young matrons, middle-aged matrons, a few displaying the respectable white hairs of age; stout women, thin women, and 'betwix' an' betweens,' as those who held a middle course between the two conditions, described themselves; some minus their boots, which they had discarded to attain greater speed, others having their skirts kilted half-way to their knees with the same object, were ranged in an extended row across the field. At the dropping of the handkerchief off they flew, vigorous white-stockinged legs flashing over the grass, loosened hair and petticoats streaming in the wind, and amid the laughter and cheers of the bystanders they reached the goal – all save a poor-spirited halfdozen who fell out at the very commencement to sink upon the turf and fan their heated faces, while they declared tht they only started to 'hearten up 'tothers so as 'um shouldn't feel shy-like.' For their part, they 'thanked the Lord that they could buy whativer calica they wanted'.

66

ROYAL OAK, WALTHAM ST LAWRENCE

Notwithstanding these lofty sentiments, the enunciators thereof regarded the winner of the despised trophy with jaundiced eyes when she returned panting but triumphant. She was a small wry woman whose six sons – imps of mischief, every one – had given her abundant practice in running, and who, when congratulated on her success, replied: 'If they tother oomans had axed my bwoys, they could ha' telled 'um 'twurn't a mossel o' use fur they to run agin I. An' if it comes to that, I reckon as I could mek a good few men look foolish!'

The fun and frolic in the meadow were kept up so long as daylight lasted. Only when night fell did the crowd melt away to seek some point of vantage, whence they might view the circle of flame-tipped hills that girt the vale with a ring of fire.

Eleanor Hayden

QUEEN VICTORIA'S JUBILEE

We lived in a comfortable Georgian farmhouse, and I was number three in a family of ten children.

My earliest recollection is the terrible snow-storm of 1881, when the teams which had gone to market had to be dug out of the snow-drifts. When they finally reached home the carters were nearly shrammed (frozen) and came into the kitchen and drank warm beer, while some of the other men gave the horses a drench of warm beer and rubbed them down with wisps of straw till they were dry. I believe the snow lay on the ground for weeks; and I remember seeing the lane, which led up to the church, being full of snow to the top of the hedges, where it had drifted in. I motored down that lane recently and remembered the snow!

My next early memory is of Queen Victoria's Jubilee in 1887, when she had been fifty years a Queen. All of us except the babies were taken to the market town (nine miles away) where all the inhabitants were given a free dinner. It was in June, and as usual with Queen Victoria, a lovely summer day. People always talked of 'Queen's weather'.

Tables were placed all down the streets next to the pavements, leaving room for the procession and bands which paraded before the feast began. All the houses were decorated with flags, and tubs were placed at intervals, and posts were fixed in them to support festoons of evergreen. It was a gay sight, and the holiday mood was everwhere. We went to a second-floor room in a house in the market-place, where a friend of my father's – an auctioneer – had his offices. It was a wonderful spot for seeing everything, and to us country children a day to be remembered, as it truly had been!

The Mayor and Corporation of the ancient Borough, who had first attended a Thanksgiving Service in the Parish Church, led the procession with the town band, and all the important burgesses. Then came the decorated carts and carriages, people on foot and on horseback in fancy dress – a gay spectacle.

THEALE

When this had all paraded the town, the dinner began. The Rector said grace and everybody sang God Save the Queen. Husbands and wives sat together – the children having teas a little later. Huge joints of beef with vegetables disappeared rapidly, followed by 'gurt big figgetty puddens' – otherwise, plum puddings. Large casks of beer stood at intervals down the street and all adults had as much as they liked, and as one can imagine the fun grew fast and furious – but we were taken home before that!

Ten years later, 1897, the Queen had her Diamond Jubilee. We were older then and helped with the celebrations in our own village. They took place in the Squire's park. Feasting again was the outstanding thing. Again it was 'Queen's weather', and the afternoon was given up to Sports, and I (always a tomboy) won the 100-yards race for girls. I would bet anyone a shilling they would never guess what the prize was – 20 yards of unbleached calico which had been bought for the tablecloths!

There were three-legged races, sack races, and a wonderful obstacle race. When the fun was over the women and children were loaded up into wagons by the farm carters and taken back to their homes – tired but happy. Although I suppose none of the people celebrating had ever seen the Queen except in pictures, she was a very real person to them all. They were intensely loyal and patriotic.

Jane Taylor

WINDSOR DIARY 1893

September 19
Sent for the doctor this morning and forthwith began to recover. Am much better tonight though decidedly weak . . .

September 20
Doctor came this morning, looked at my tongue and said it was very good, felt my pulse and said it was alright, said I need not take any more of the medicine and I would soon be well. Suggested that 'a little brandy' would be desirable in my water at meals, for which advice I thanked him, but, of course, shall take the water neat . . . he does not intend calling again.

Alexander Elliot

SMOCKS AND STOCKS

Many and many a happy hour may the fisherman spend upon the banks of the Lambourne. Should he be fortunate enough to find himself in the valley in June, he will probably return home with a heart at peace with the world and a full basket, for trout are numerous in the little river, and leafy June is the best month of all for the sport. A few days' fishing, in the valley during the months of July, August, or September, is an

BRAY

amusement by no means to be despised by those who appreciate the sport.

High up above the villages upon either side lie the Berkshire Downs, sunny and bright and pleasant in summer and autumn; bleak and dreary enough in winter when the wind sweeps over them, and the snow hides all traces of the tracks and footpaths, the only signs of human life.

Now and then a wagon will appear upon the skyline, and move slowly along the ridge, or a group of gleaners working in the harvest-fields. All the women wear the old-fashioned sunbonnets. Now and then, a year or two ago, a smock-frock might actually have been seen, few and far between indeed, perhaps only two or three remaining in the whole of the valley. Even the oldest men have given them up; 'they have grown too proud,' an old woman said to me rather sadly one day. Her husband had given up wearing his before he died, but she 'did like to see him in it when it was washed and clean.' Being of a frugal mind, and apparently not sharing the pride with which she accredited her husband, she had cut it up and made it into a 'wropper' for herself, and 'a beautiful wropper it had made.'

Strange when one thinks of it, this discontinuance of the smock-frock. Has the need for it departed, with the decrease of human agricultural labour, and the increase of machinery, or is the reason for its disuse to be found simply in a change of

UFFINGTON

69

THAMES EEL TRAPS, READING

fashion? Is it really, as the old woman in the Lambourne valley said, that the men have grown too proud to wear them, or is it not quite possible that the fault lay partly with the women, who no longer possessed the patience required for making them. The beautiful needlework which went to the fashioning of these old country garments needed plenty of that admirable virtue; the smock-frock was not made in a day. Whatever the reason for its departure, it has gone; and when one visits the picturesque villages that now know it no more, one cannot help regretting its absence. For it would still well fit into the picture.

But here, while bemoaning its loss, I must record a delightful instance of its still being worn in one little town in the north of Berkshire. There, if you happen to be fortunate, you may catch a glimpse of an old dairyman said to be in affluent circumstances, looking as if he had stepped straight out of a picture of Morland's – smock-frock, low felt hat, yoke upon his shoulders with shining milk buckets hanging from it, all complete. Ellen Terry once, when driving through this quaint little town, saw his picturesque figure, and her artistic eye was at once delighted. Stopping the carriage, she eagerly asked where the smocks could be bought, and – the story goes – supplied herself with two or three. From somewhere, I presume they must still be obtainable, for the old dairyman's cannot last for ever, but one has an uncomfortable suspicion that now they may be machine-made. After all, different times, dif-

ferent manners; other changes have taken place also. The same old woman who regretted the smock, and whose age was lost in the midst of years, remembered the village stocks. This discontinuance she did not regret. She had often seen them used, and an old man in the village told a similar story. This old fellow appeared to have considered himself of some importance in the place, for he had often mounted guard over the unfortunate victims of these instruments of torture. The offenders, according to their former guardian, had to sit upon the ground, not a pleasant position certainly, in damp or wet weather. Visions of all sorts of future ills, that those prisoners were laying up for themselves, passed rapidly before my mind's eye – colds and coughs, and bronchitis, and pneumonia, to say nothing of the seeds of a whole crop of greater ills. One's pity might just as well be reserved for some more serious object. Things were better than they appeared; the wind was tempered to the shorn lamb, even in the stocks. A moment later, with a knowing twinkle in his eye, seeing my distressful countenance, the old man went on to say, 'We generally gave them something to sit upon; we couldn't be too hard.' Alas! how soon all personal memory of these things will have passed away, and with it, I think, much of the interest and picturesqueness of these old-world villages.

L.S.

THE WATER CARRIER

FISHING IN THE THAMES, READING

TROUT AND CRAYFISH

The little river Enbourne divides the county of Hampshire from that of Berkshire. At Hyde End, which is a hamlet of Brimpton, and lies just within the latter county, the dreamy sleepiness of the little river has been interfered with and its course somewhat diverted. A trout farm has been established there, and stews made to contain the fish in various stages of their development. The spawn is kept in narrow ducts; afterwards, when grown to sufficient size, the fish are drafted off into the enclosed portions of the river, finally being despatched by rail in special cans, very like those that milk is sent in; not to be eaten — at least not yet — but to stock streams and river, doubtless to be caught again eventually.

The care and culture of the trout is no sinecure, for the river must be carefully watched; it must not be too high nor too low. If it rises too high the fish run the risk of being flooded, and finally left high and dry upon the banks. While, on the other hand, if the water sinks too low, this is equally dangerous for the fish. A most ingenious electric contrivance rings two bells in the old mill where the fishery-keeper lives, to give warning of either of these contingencies happening. The trout have many enemies, too; one of the worst, alas! is supposed to be the kingfisher. The keeper is not merciful should he happen to have his gun when the brilliant little emerald-green body flashes past towards the sedges. The destruction of this most beautiful of English birds, now rapidly becoming rare, is very sad; it weighs heavily in the scales against pisciculture.

Should you happen to be at the fishery at feeding time, you will find it an amusing and interesting performance. The food — not a pleasant-looking concoction — is minced and chopped-up horseflesh. A horrible idea seizes one that those two broken-down old horses, so happily munching the grass in the field close by, are getting ready, and only waiting their turn to produce a further supply of the commodity. Never mind, do not think of it; the horses are contented and happy now, their end will be merciful, doubtless — and fishes must be fed. In their manner of feeding is found a vast difference. The common brown, or Loch Leven troutlets, feed quietly, accepting whatever happens to come, without any show of eagerness whatsoever. Slow, placid sort of fellows they are, taking life easily, and troubling themselves apparently very little about it. With the other species, the rainbow trout, it is all a very different matter. He is a restless, excitable creature, and darts greedily at his food, flashing and flickering to the surface, twisting his body rapidly, so that the light catches it. And as hundreds, or even thousands, of them are all doing the same thing at the same moment, the water has the appearance of an ever-moving kaleidoscope of silver and iridescent tint. The natures and temperaments of fish are evidently just as differing as are the natures and temperaments of human beings.

The trout that breeds naturally in the Enbourne is small, but the pike grow to a fine size. One shellfish, however, which has either become scarce, or absent altogether from other rivers, is always to be found in this Berkshire stream. I mean the crayfish. Do you know them? — funny, uncanny, lobster-like crea-

BLADE BONE INN, BUCKLEBURY

tures that they are. I do not mean in the fishmonger's shops, after they have been boiled and turned scarlet, or when they are brought to table. But do you know them alive, and mud-coloured? have you made their acquaintance in their native haunts? in short, have you ever been upon a crayfishing expedition? If you never have, come with me. It will be a new experience for you.

Crayfishing must be done when it is dark; the fish will not move much in the day-time; we must not start till towards dusk. We will take the little cart and the old donkey, for the nets are heavy to carry; we can take the cart right down into the fields, and tie the donkey to a gate-post till we have finished. The rest of the party will walk, or go on their bicycles. The nets are put into the cart; the bait – well, that some obliging garden or stable boy has attended to; it is not a pleasant process. Crayfish are fond of liver that has 'hung' for some indefinite period; they love savoury meat.

So we start, through the darkening lanes. Now and then a belated labourer, whose work has taken him far from home, wishes us 'Good-night.' The donkey – as is the manner of his kind – is somewhat erratic in his movements, occasionally going at a hand-gallop, afterwards relapsing into a slow walk. It does not matter: there is no hurry, the evening is warm and delicious, and going at a slow pace is no hardship.

WILTS AND BERKS CANAL, WANTAGE

NEWBURY

The last of the light has faded, dusk is growing into darkness, the stars are beginning to appear as we turn into the fields. Thump, bump, with a good deal of jolting over some deep ruts; through a gateway, across a field of very uneven going, through another gateway, over some more ruts, which have recently been full of water and soft mud, but now are dry and rough, and we have arrived at our destinies. Near the river the grass is long; very soon, if we are to have a fine day on the morrow, it will be wet, so for a crayfishing expedition it is necessary to have thick boots.

Leaving the donkey to its own devices, having secured it to a post, we cross the field towards the river, if river it can be called, for it is really nothing more than a little stream, almost hidden by bushes and the high grassy banks beneath which it has sunk. Upon these banks here and there may be found the beautiful American balsam (*Impatiens bicolor*), now become naturalised, with its bright orange-coloured flowers, so much more showy than most of the English field-flowers.

The overgrown pools are the best places for cray-fishing, though the movements of crayfish are undependable. Sometimes they will frequent one particular pool, sometimes

another; you can never be quite sure where you will find them. Neither can you be certain whether you will have good sport or bad. Crayfish are moody creatures; for some unknown reason of their own, if they are not so inclined, even the most savoury morsel will fail to please them. Occasionally they have been known to resist the temptations of the best 'hung' and most gamey piece of meat.

Having chosen a spot that seems likely, a deep dark pool, overhung with trees upon the farther side, we make our first venture. The net is suspended over the water by a long crooked stick, the string being gradually paid out over it. There is a soft, almost inaudible splash; weighted by its iron ring, the flat net sinks to the bottom. Another net is lowered, a little farther off, then another and another, till all our ventures are made. Nothing is left to do now but wait. Fishing always means waiting, and waiting means patience, and patience of all virtues is the most unornamental and the hardest to attain. But patience sometimes wins its reward. Perhaps it will be so in the case of our crayfishing. Meanwhile, it is better to wait in silence, or, at any rate, to talk quietly. Crayfish are reported, with what measures of truth it is difficult to say,

74

THAMES LOCK, COOKHAM

to be afraid of the human voice. And nature keeps us company in silence. Now and then a grasshopper raises his small voice, to make the silence more intense; sometimes a bird rustles in the branches, or you hear the heavy breathing of the cows that are feeding at the farther end of the field. Now we may venture to prove our luck. We will begin with the first net that was lowered, and so on one after another. We should never find the line at all were it not for the little piece of rag that is tied to the end of each of them and lies like a white butterfly upon the bank for a guide. With breathless suspense the first net is hauled up; a rustling noise proceeding from it as it comes near proclaims that there is something in it. A moment later and a hep of little mud-coloured creatures with wriggling bodies and fighting claws are lying on the ground. You must pick them up by the middle of their backs if you do not want a sharp pinch; those little nippers would soon make the fact very forcibly known that you cannot handle a crayfish anyhow with impunity. So one net after another is taken out of the water; in some there are fish, some come to land empty. Now and again an annoying thing happens: just as the net is lifted out of the water, over it will tip; with a splash, back goes a crayfish home again. Perhaps it was the result of clumsiness, perhaps that particular crayfish bore a charmed life – who can tell? If he is wise he will resist the temptations of a highly seasoned but unknown meal for the future.

It is curious, sometimes, that a superstition will continue in the face of all evidence of its untruth. I am alluding to the saying in some parts of the country that if you take a crayfish out of the water the stream will dry up. Over and over again this saying must obviously have been proved false, yet in spite of this you may still occasionally stumble across it.

We have had good sport. We can afford to let a few of the funny little mud-coloured beings escape. Now it is time to go home; we make our way under the starlight through the thick white blanket which to the height of a few feet covers the grass. It is damp and chilly; wet feet we should certainly get, were we not provided with strong country boots.

Another beautiful day will greet us on the morrow; we may thank the mist for giving us that assurance. So with the donkey, his stable in view, galloping at a pace that would mean danger should anything obstruct the path, we go recklessly through the lanes to our beds.

L.S.

ELDERBERRY WINE

'Will you 'ev some elderberry wine, or be you a teetot'ler?'

'I should like some, if you please,' I said. So she fetched out a small jug of the wine, and warmed it over the fire, as is usual with this kind of drink, and reached down a tin of biscuits from between a set of ancient brass candlesticks standing on the mantelpiece, and granny gently and shyly pushed a big orange into my hand, while Tommy sat smiling, and thrumming on the table with his fingers.

SHEEP FAIR, EAST ILSLEY

Elderberry wine is a wholesome drink, and stands high in the estimation of the villagers. The berries are gathered when ripe, and placed in cold water; after soaking for several days they are boiled down, and the liquor strained off and sweetened; the wine, taken warm at bedtime, is good to cure a cold. Besides the wine, there is also elderberry jam, or the fruit is used to make tarts and pies, and is sometimes preserved in syrup, as with greengages; some of the old-fashioned sort of people always make an elderberry pie with fruit kept in this way at Christmas. Another use of the elder is that of making a wash for the skin, by steeping the bunches of bloom in boiling water; it is said to be very efficacious in removing freckles and beautifying the complexion.

Alfred Williams

A BERKSHIRE SHEEP-FAIR

East Ilsley is a queer little village. At first sight it really appears to consist almost entirely of public-houses. They are The Star, The Lamb, The White Hart, The Wheatsheaf, The Swan, The White Horse, and The Crown and Horns, besides two or three others. All these in the single street of a little village whose population has never been more than eight hundred, and has now dwindled down to only five hundred. It really sounds rather alarming. East Ilsley, you think, must surely be a place to be avoided – what can the people be like? Wait a minute; if you are thus hasty in your judgment you will be doing the poor innocent Ilsleyites a grievous wrong. They are probably no better and no worse than the inhabitants of any other village. The reason for this extraordinary predominance of public-houses is not to be found in any unusual vice upon their part, or to any peculiar addiction to drink; it is due to something quite different, – the existence of the sheep-fairs. The sheep-fair of East Ilsley is one of the most important and one of the most ancient in England. The charter for its establishment was granted as long ago as the reign of Henry III, and, as the public-houses would not exist were it not for the sheep-fairs, so the sheep-fairs could not possibly get on at all without the public-houses. Over the Downs and from far away the shepherds have to travel and drive their sheep, and as the fair begins early in the morning most of the sheep must be there the night before, and the shepherds and the drovers have

SHEEP FAIR, EAST ILSLEY

to sleep somewhere. So they flock within the hospitable doors of The Star, The Lamb, and The White Horse — and thus the necessity of the public-houses is accounted for.

The chief fair takes place annually upon August 1st. You must be at East Ilsley by nine o'clock in the morning if you wish to see it in full swing. It is a sight that is well worth an effort of early rising. Perhaps it is a grey day; one of those delicious mornings of late summer when every line is softened, and every tint deepened, and the most commonplace object is rendered beautiful by a veil of haze. As far as the eye can see lie the Downs, bearing upon their bosom an infinity of colour and shade. Golden cornfields, with huge patches of yellow charlock in between, farther on a perfect blaze of scarlet poppies with perhaps a white chalk-pit gleaming near. Encircling it all, the purple line of the everlasting hills, broken here and there by an irregular tuft of trees against the sky. As you wind along the road on your bicycle, or in your motor perhaps (though one must confess the thought even of a motor seems terribly out of place in connection with an East Ilsley sheep fair), the bleating of sheep and the barking of dogs tells you that you are approaching the fair. Join the long string of vehicles of every description going in the same direction, swing round a sharp corner, and you will find yourself in the village.

Just at the corner, one of the first things that meets one's eye is a little butcher's shop — not the ordinary one, which certain-ly could not be called a picturesque object, but a quaint little wooden erection, with its front painted bright green, reminding one curiously of childhood's days, carrying one's memory back to a certain fascinating toy with painted legs of mutton, sirloins of beef, and a little wooden butcher standing at the door with a miniature chopper in his hand. Farther on, this illusion of memory is rendered still more complete. For the small square pens into which the sheep are packed are for all the world like the pens of a mimic farmyard. The crowded, bulky, motionless sheep might so well be those delightful wooden animals, from which one used to be scolded for sucking the paint, because — dreadful thought — that paint was probably poisonous. Still the illusion continues. Stand at the bottom of the hill upon which East Ilsley is built and gaze up the little street, at the quaint buildings and perspective of rudely painted signs swinging from the fronts of the inns. Are you not reminded of those old childish picture-books, John Gilpin, The House that Jack Built, and the rest, long ago consigned to the limbo of all forgotten things. To hear sheep bleating is said to be a sign of loss, while, apparent contradiction, to find oneself surrounded by them is lucky, so with this portent of good luck awaiting us, we will hurry on.

In the village all is bustle and life. More than twenty thousand sheep are enclosed in pens upon either side of the street, stretching out, a woolly mass, towards the fields behind. Their

CEMETERY ROAD JUNCTION, READING

number lately has been reduced by about one-half from what it formerly was – the result of the agricultural depression. Every species of sheep is represented. There are the Hampshire Downs, the Sussex and Wiltshire, and a handsome Scotch breed having horns. Thousands of sheep are bleating, hundreds of dogs are barking loudly, some of them held by the shepherds who are watching over the sheep; others are tied to the pens whilst their owners go a little way off to gossip with their friends, or make a voyage of discovery through the fair. The dogs are chiefly of the collie breed; here and there is conspicuous a great English sheep-dog, quieter and more dignified than the somewhat fussy and sometimes mongrel collie.

It is a grey day, there is no sun to scorch, so the sheep have no need of the trees planted at intervals in all the open spaces, wherever the pens are put up. These trees are chiefly chestnuts. The beauty of the scene of a sheep-fair must be greatly increased in the spring when the trees are in blossom.

The passages in between the pens are filled with men in every variety of costume, some of the most picturesque description. Many of the drovers, with their knotted red handkerchiefs and general get-up, remind one of the London coster. Here you may see a man, one of the dealers, in a velveteen jacket and a soft felt hat, looking as though he were

dressed for the stage; there is another in a long white coat reaching to his heels, with huge gold spectacles and white hat, a cross between a bowler and a tall hat cut down. Infinite variety! But the smock-frock – one longs to see it – is, alas! absent. Nevertheless, the endless and picturesque modification which the English costume, prosaic and ugly though one is apt to consider it, seems capable of at a Berkshire sheep-fair is surprising.

One old shepherd, who carries the invariable heavy walking-stick that appears to have taken the place of the shepherd's crook, wears a dark-blue smocked coat and a slouch hat. His face bears the calm and beautiful expression that is seen sometimes upon the faces of those old shepherds whose whole life has been spent with Nature, alone, in the fields or upon the Downs, with no companionship but that of their sheep and their dogs, when they would wile away the time of their solitude sometimes in carving wonderful designs upon walking-sticks. Now and then in an old house you may see one of these sticks; and an interesting piece of workmanship it is. This man's whole bearing is a combination of quiet dignity and childlike simplicity. When a snapshot photograph was taken of him and his great shaggy bob-tailed dog, he came up immediately afterwards expecting to see his likeness; his face clouded

BERKSHIRE SHEPHERDS

STATUE OF KING ALFRED, WANTAGE

over with disappointment when he was told that a great deal
had yet to be done before the picture came into existence.

That fine old man; one could imagine his desiring to have
carried out at his death the almost obsolete custom of placing
a lock of the sheep's wool in the shepherd's coffin, in order
that at the Judgment Day his calling might be known, and thus
a reason given for his irregular attendance at church during his
lifetime. The simple pathos of the ancient custom might well
attach itself to this particular old shepherd.

Presently an unusually loud bleating of sheep and barking of
dogs is heard. What can be happening? The fair is nearly over,
and a flock of sheep is being driven, or rather is refusing to be
driven, away. Sheep are said to have an instinctive and curious
objection to going downhill upon an unknown road. These
particularl animals are exhibiting this trait to an amazing
extent. A rope has been fastened round the neck of one of
them and the victim is thus being dragged along, in the hope
that, sheep-like, the others will follow. Nothing of the kind.
The hope is altogether a vain one, their conduct is most
unsheep-like. They rush and bound about in every direction,
they even leap the hurdles, and get mixed up with the others.
About twenty dogs are now yapping at their heels, evidently
thinking it all fine fun. One dog seizes a shepherd by the leg,
doubtless in his excitement mistaking him for a sheep. The
noise is deafening, the dust is sent flying in smothering clouds.
Headlong rush the sheep – in ever direction but the one in

which they are intended to go, scattering the men, who are
powerless to stem the torrent of their mad flight. In the end
the sheep get their own way, and go down another road, leading, however, by a circuitous route to the one by which they
were originally intended to go.

L.S.

BERKSHIRE CHERRIES

This part of the country is famed for its cherries, and grows
them to a large extent. Formerly, the fruit was gathered by the
occupier of the orchard, and sold to small dealers, who came
in their carts from Newbury, Hungerford, Marlborough, and
other distant towns, and if the villager were early astir on these
occasions, he could purchase cherries – the choicest of them –
at twopence per pound. Now however the orchards are sold *en
bloc*, and the wholesale customer engages his own men to
gather and pack the fruit.

When the berries are ripening, the sound of guns is heard
from sunrise to sunset.

'It is like living in a besieged place,' a newcomer remarked;
men or boys being stationed in every orchard to fire at the
birds, who otherwise would leave little fruit to come to the
hammer.

CHERRY PICKERS, HARWELL

The following cherry story, if not ture, is at least *ben trovato*. Mr. A———, a man of substance in the neighbourhood, and the owner of several orchards, conceived a fancy many years since to visit Paris. Thither accordingly he journeyed, and seeing one day during his perambulations some fine cherries exposed for sale in a shop window, he went in and inquired the price. They were a franc a pound – a sum the farmer thought excessive. 'But they are English,' explained the proprietor. This aroused Mr. A———'s curiosity, and he asked from what part of England they came. 'From a place called Berkshire,' was the reply. Further investigation showed that they were the product of the village where he lived, probably from one of his own orchards. The story does not say whether he bought them back at more than three times the amount for which he sold them!

Eleanor Hayden

Skill Of The Farm Labourer

An old farmer aged eighty-six told me that in his young days farmers used to employ a couple of maids and two men and a boy, or two boys and a man. They received five shillings a week, lived in the farm-house, had everything found for them, including cider and beer brewed on the farm. There were no amusements, no means for spending money, no cinemas or theatres or public-houses; and scores of them saved their money, bought and stocked a small farm, and many of them became large farmers and successful men. They knew their business, and the girls they married knew theirs, and could milk and make butter and cheese and cider, and cook, and harness a horse, and make a first-rate farmer's wife, and rear a lusty family of strong, healthy children for the good of posterity. The agricultural labourer does not need to be taught a smattering of drawing, of English literature and various 'ologies. It is good for him that his mind should be trained as well as his body; but the pursuit of agriculture is a wonderful mind-trainer, if a boy really tries to learn. The work of the factory hand is often purely mechanical, requiring little intelligence. I have seen one man in a biscuit factory spending his days in directing with two fingers the course of certain biscuits as they emerge from the machine from one plate to another, a task, continuously performed, enough to drive the worker into a lunatic asylum. Whereas in agriculture all is varied; there is little mechanical about it. In ploughing, the weather, the depth of the furrow, its straightness, the management of the horses, all vary, and its pursuit cultivates intelligence and is far removed from the monotony of a machine-minding existence.

WILLIAM WING AND FRIENDS AT THE ROEBUCK INN, TILEHURST

A ploughman has before him a tremendous task. He has to draw straight lines through a field with a troublesome instrument called a plough with the aid of still more troublesome agents called horses; and I look with admiration upon a field newly ploughed by a skilful ploughman. The furrows are as straight as a die. This is skilled labour. Contrast it with the work of a machine worker, or a driver on a tube railway who presses a button and the thing works itself and cannot go wrong.

Peter Ditchfield

THAMES VALLEY BY CARAVAN

There is to my way of thinking a delicious uncertainty in starting on a long caravan tour, without being aware in the least what you are going to do or see, or even what route you are going to take.

As regards a route, though, I did throw up a pebble with a black tick on it before the horses pulled out at the gate, and twice running the spot pointed to the north-west.

So we steered for Reading, and on without stopping as far as the Roebuck Hotel at Tilehurst. Nine years ago this hotel

was a very small one indeed, but all gables, thickest thatch, and climbing roses and honeysuckle. The thatch has given place to red tiles, and an addendum of modern dimensions has been built. The old must ever give place to the new. But what lovely peeps there are from this hotel, from the balcony and from the bedrooms. It is a river house now in every sense of the word, though not old as a hotel of the kind, and all day long, and far into the night, the bar and passages and the coffee-rooms are crowded in summer with men in snowy flannels, and with some in sailor garb and with artificial sailor swagger.

The road leads onwards through a cool elm avenue towards Pangbourne. The copses here are in earlier spring carpeted with wild hyacinths. On the hill-top the scenery opens out again, the tree-clad valley of the Thames, fields of green grain, with poppies here and there, or wild mustard, and fields crimson with blossoming trefoil. Surely milk and butter must be good when cows are fed on flowers.

'Lay till the day' in the great inn yard of the George. Rather too close to the railway embankment, for the trains went roaring past all night long. This did not make sleeping impossible, for a gipsy, even an amateur one, can sleep anywhere; but the earth shook and the lamps rattled every time a train rolled by. Some villas are built right beneath the embankment, which is far higher than their roofs. What a

strange and terrible accident it would be were one of those trains to leave the line and run through a roof! An old lady of the nervous persuasion who lives here told me that she often-times trembled in her bed when she thought of this dread possibility.

Pangbourne is a well-known haunt for those who love boating and fishing. It is quiet, and so well shaded as to be cool on the warmest summer day. But Pangbourne is not a hackneyed place, and never, I believe, will be so.

June 19th

Left about nine o'clock. It had been raining just enough to lay the dust and give a brighter colouring to the foliage.

Ivy leaves, when young, are of a very bright green. There are on a well-kept lawn by the riverside, and just outside Pangbourne, a coach-house and a boathouse. Both are well built and prettily shaped. They are thatched, and the walls are completely covered in close-cropped ivy, giving them the look of houses built of green leaves.

Two miles from Pangbourne a nice view of the Thames valley is obtained, round wooded hills on the right bank, with farms here and there, and fields now covered with waving wheat, some of them flooded over with the rich red of the blossoming sainfoin.

We reach the village of Lower Basildon. Spring seems to linger long in this sweet vale. Here is a lofty spruce, each twiglet pointed with a light green bud; here a crimson flowered chestnut; yonder a row of pink mays and several laburnums, whose drooping blooms show no symptoms yet of fading or falling.

At the grotto we pass through a splendid avenue of beeches.

Just at the top of a steep hill-top we meet a girl and a boy on the same tricycle. How happy they look! We warn them of the steepness of the descent. They smilingly thank us, put on their brake, and go floating away and finally disappear among the beeches.

Every one has rushed through Goring and Streatley by train, and some may have thought the villages pretty. So they are indeed, but you must go by road to find this out. Look at them from Grotto Hill, for instance, just after you emerge from the lane.

Here is a pretty bit of road. On the left is a high bank covered with young beech-trees, a hedge on the right, then a green field sweeping down the hill to the river's edge. The Thames is here bordered with willow-trees and flowering elders. That hedgerow is low and very wild. It may be blackthorn at heart, but it is quite encanopied by a wealth of trailing weeds and flowers, and by roses and honeysuckle all in bloom, while the roadsides are laid out by nature's hand in beds of yellow trefoil and blue speedwell. The pink marshmallow, too, is growing in every grassy nook by the hedgefoot.

I wonder how far on my journey north will hedgerows accompany me. I shall feel sorry when they give place to unsightly wooden fences or walls of rugged stone.

High up yonder is a green grassy tableland or moor, through which goes the ancient ridge-way or cattle-road to Wales. Unused now, of course, but the scene of many a strange story in bygone times.

PANGBOURNE

A little very old man gets out from under a tree and stands as straight as he can to gaze at us. Surely the oldest inhabitant of these regions. His dress is peculiar – a cow-gown worn beneath and protruding like a kilt from under a long blue coat, and a tall black hat. He bobs his wrinkled face, grins, and talks to himself as we pass. A queer old man indeed.

We stopped on Moulsford Hill to water horses. A fine open country, and breezy to-day. Rather too breezy, in fact, for hardly had we started again before the wind got in under the great awning which covers the roof from stem to stern. It ripped the cloth from the hooks that held it, but I caught it in time, else it would have blown over the horses' heads, and might have given rise to a very serious accident.

It was market day at Wallingford, and busy and bustling it was in the little town. The place is close to the Thames. It boasts of a bridge with nineteen arches, a very ancient history, and the remains of an old castle, which, it is said, was at one time considered impregnable. It was besieged by King Stephen, and defied him. It held out against Cromwell too, I am told, and was one of the last places to surrender. The remains of its ancient walls are visible enough in the shape of mounds, turf-clad, and green as a grave. Did Wallingford not hold out against the Danes also? I believe it did. I have already had so much of Oliver Cromwell and the Danes dinned into my ear that I am heartily tired of both. If I can credit current

traditions, the Danes must have been very badly handled indeed, and must have bitterly repented ever setting a foot on English shores.

William Gordon Stables MD RN

WOOLSTONE MILL

The little village of Woolstone lies below the hill, out of sight of the coomb, nestling among tall trees of elm and beech, shut away from the outer world, undisturbed with the fierce controversies of the hour, and the burning passions that unsettle and sway the rest of mankind. The cottages are quaint and ancient – of the Elizabethan period, and earlier – with walls of brick and timber interbuilt, and thatched roofs, picturesquely set amid gardens looking out from underneath green spreading boughs. Halfway down is the romantic White Horse Inn; a short way below this the waters of the spring – now the River Ock – emerge from the neighbouring grounds and plunge down beneath the road amid large moss-covered stones, as did the beautiful Arethusa to escape the embraces of the passionate river god Alpheus in the mountains of Acroceraunia.

The old mill stands father down, a short distance from the road, at the head of a large pool well stocked with trout. It is

84

not often in requisition now, though it is used for gristing occasionally. The great wheel is contained in a shed – to protect it from the wet, as is jocularly said; the floors and beams within the mill are mouldering away to dust. Once upon a time, at a small mill on a stream in the valley, the wheel was considerably out of repair; the oscillation was so great that it shook the crockery off the kitchen shelves in the miller's cottage adjoining. So the mill-wrights came to renovate the wood-work and bearings; after three days of hard labour all was well again, and the machinery was started, unknown to the miller's wife. She, good soul, came out in the afternoon to call the workmen to tea.

'Come an in an' hae a cup o' tea, then you can finish un better,' said she.

'Bless ee, mother, 'e's finished now, an' a runnin' too, this long time,' they replied.

'Is the mill-'a-gwain?' she inquired, with astonishment.

'Gwain, aa! We ground dree sacks an' moore a'ready,' they answered.

'An' I ent a yerd a sound o' nothin'!' the miller's wife regretfully responded.

Alfred Williams

THE MILLWAY

The Millway is an offshoot from the main village street and was the abode of a little colony of aged folk before death and household 'shiftings' removed them elsewhere.

Every day the ancient dames – bent, crippled with rheumatism, and what they called 'the triatic' – would creep down through their gardens where bees were busy among the gillyflowers, to the stone step against which the water was gently lapping. Buckets would be dipped, lifted with infinite difficulty, half-filled, to land and carried home, a labour necessitating several halts on the way, although the distance was not great.

Sarah Toomer who with her husband, lived in the cottage nearest the stream, made a practice of feeding the trout during the summer months, for which she was liberally rewarded by the farmer whose visitors from London reaped the benefit of her forethought when they rented the fishing on the opposite bank.

The Toomers' neighbour was not without a certain claim to distinction: she felt that she possessed an almost proprietary right in the brook, being intimately conneted with water.

'My son, 'ee knaw,' she would explain with pardonable pride, 'a lives up at Barrow: 'tis a ter'ble girt way off, an' folks sez you've got to crass the water to get to't. I cassn't say myself, fur I've niver bin ther'; but that's as 'tis. My son drives an engine; not one o' them as runs on rails an' screeches fit to mammer arrabody. His'n be what you calls a drudge – sommat as clanes out the sea, luk 'ee. I reckon that 'ull be a longish job, so ther' ben't much fear o' him bein' short o' work yet awhiles. Dear, dear, who'd ha' thought as iver the sea could ha' bin claned out? but ther's no tellin' what folks wun't be up to nowadays!'

This old lady was chained to her fireside by the complaint so common among working women – namely, 'a bad leg' and

'THE WILLOWS', TWYFORD

that of the most virulent type. If it were poor Hannah's cross, it was at the same time her pride and glory. Nothing afforded her greater pleasure than to exhibit to a luckless visitor the ghastly spectacle of her 'pooer dear 'ounded limb,' and she derived a singular satisfaction from the thought that 'it 'ud be despert hard to find a wusser leg nor mine.' It would indeed have been difficult to have imagined such a one. Notwithstanding the constant pain she suffered, she was ever cheerful and when I visited her, would tell me of the good old times when her father earned five shillings a week and her mother made 'tea' from burnt crusts, so that a blackened loaf was a welcome sight.

Eleanor Hayden

BLEWBURY JOKERS

Practical jokes were constantly being played. Some of these jokes, it is true, were of a cruel and dangerous nature, and society certainly benefits by their discontinuance. On the other hand, many were harmless, and contained a certain spice of humour, rough and ready, no doubt, but humour nevertheless. And a good hearty laugh at an innocent joke that hurt nobody must have been good for the village people, I think.

However, be that as it may, I fancy that old Martin, upon whom one of these practical jokes was played, in the end probably joined in the laugh against himself. He was an old basket-maker, who went round from place to place and farm to farm to repair anything of the nature of wicker-work, sieves or baskets, or chairs, that chanced to be broken. One day he arrived at a certain farm, tied up his pony and cart, and was busily engaged upon the various articles requiring his attention which were brought to him by the different labourers. Now, it so happened that these labourers had an idle time just then, it being too wet for them to get upon the land for ploughing. So, while old Martin was busily at work, it occurred to them that the basket-maker might be made the subject of some fun. They found his pony tied to a door-handle happily munching a meal of coarse hay. Their first act was to unharness the animal from the cart; then they removed the wheels from it, after which, by dint of a good deal of turning and twisting, the body of the cart was got inside the barn. Their next piece of work was to put the wheels back upon the cart and harness the pony, after which they all climbed up and hid themselves in the *tallet*, prepared to thoroughly enjoy the sport when old Martin came and found out what had happened. They had to wait for some time, but not long enough to cool their ardour in the anticipation of the fun. Presently old Martin's work was finished, and he wished to get on to the next farm. Great was

86

WALLINGFORD

his dismay when neither pony nor cart could be found. After a vain search he peeped inside the barn, and joyfully discovered his lost property. Then came the problem how to get the horse and cart out of the barn; if it had gone in, it could be got out again; but, then, how it got in remained a mystery, and how to get it out again was an equal one. Old Martin gave it up: it was beyond his powers of solution. At last a loud laugh resounding from the *tallet* proclaimed the fact that he was not alone, and the young labourers, thoroughly satisfied with the success of their joke, climbed down to the old man's assistance.

A victim of a somewhat similar and equally innocent kind of prank was a certain Malachi Grace, who kept the New Inn at Blewbury. Malachi, who was a carrier to Wallingford, had an unfortunate propensity for visiting inns other than his own upon the road – unfortunate because, though the visits in themselves were harmless enough, Malachi found it necessary to do a great deal for the good of the house he visited, which was to his own detriment. One day he had been feeling particularly sociable, and the consequence was that presently the horse was leisurely making his way homewards, stopping occasionally to munch the grass by the roadside, while all the time the master reposed peacefully at the bottom of the van fast asleep. The situation was discovered by some young labourers, who, ready and willing for a joke, took the horse out of the van, drew the latter with Malachi still asleep in it into a barn, and secreted themselves to watch for developments. Presently

it grew dark, Malachi woke up, rubbed his eyes, looked about him, and gave utterance to the following somewhat cryptic remark: 'Is my name Malachi Grace? Because if it is I've lost a horse; if 't'aint, I've found a cart.'

But the playing of practical jokes was by no means confined to the labourers; the following is the story of one, the author of which was a Blewbury farmer and the victim a tailor of the same village. This tailor had received an order from a neighbouring squire to make him a particular kind of shooting coat. It was to contain a number of specially large pockets to hold game, for in those days sportsmen carried their own bag, not considering a man to do so for them a necessary adjunct to a day's shooting. The order received by the tailor was apparently one of unusual importance, and was much boasted of amongst his friends and customers. Amongst the latter was a young farmer, who, as the tailor had happened to mention to him the day and hour arranged for the fitting on of the coat, determined to have some amusement. He waited for the man to pass his house with the wonderful coat in a parcel, and called out to him over the hedge, 'My missus wants you to measure one of the children for a suit of clothes.' Delighted with the prospect of another order, the tailor went into the house, put his parcel down in the hall, and was shown into a room, where he spent some minutes in measuring the farmer's little boy. Meanwhile the farmer quickly undid the parcel, abstracted the wonderful coat, and substituted for it one of his wife's flannel

BEENHAM

petticoats. Later, arrived at the squire's, the tailor proceeded to unpack the parcel, his face beaming all the time with conscious pride while he dilated upon the merits of the marvellous garment. He was sure the squire would be pleased with it; he had put a pocket here and a pocket there; the thing when finished would be an enormous success. The parcel was opened; the change of expression upon the tailor's face took place more rapidly than can be described. 'I'll drop it into my apprentice, young rascal!' he spluttered, purple with rage. 'I'll teach him to play me jokes like this!' And off he went as fast as his legs would carry him, intending to give the apprentice an unpleasant time of it. The farmer was on the look-out for him. 'My missus wants you to measure the other little boy,' he called out, as the tailor hurried past, fuming with suppressed fury. Here was balm in Gilead. The tailor halted, the apprentice and the meditated vengeance were forgotten for a few minutes. He went into the house and proceeded to take the order. In the meantime the farmer took the flannel petticoat out of the parcel, returned the coat, and tied it up again. The tailor hurried forth presently again, hurling expletives at the head of the innocent apprentice. It was no use his professing ignorance of the matter; the proof of his impudence was here – here in the parcel; the coat had been taken out and the flannel petticoat, &c., &c. With fingers that trembled with fury he untied the string. Let us hope for his own sake that the mysti-

fied apprentice made good his escape at the opportune moment and at any rate indulged in his laughter in private.

L.S.

ETONIANS AT FROGMORE

It was officially notified to us (at Eton) that Queen Charlotte desired to see the boys at a game of cricket, and so a first-class eleven was meted out. The Queen sat in state on the broad terrace before the house, with a long line of her daughters and ladies standing on each side of her, with the Prince Regent, for a while, leaning his hand on the back of her chair, and talking with her. Behind were a troop of aides-de-camp and others – a brilliant Court.

The Eleven played their best, and right proudly. To be bowled out, or caught, would have been as a life's misfortune; and this had gone on for some twenty minutes or so, when the Princess Augusta, standing by the Queen, and seeing the players cross each other, run, and hit and throw about a ball, turned to the lady next to her, and remarking that it was rather dull, asked 'When are the boys going to begin?'

W.H. Tucker

WRIGHT'S MEADOW, UFFINGTON

THE QUAKER MEETING

A children's game in which players sing the song whilst gathering together sufficient numbers for the play.
The children sing:

> Would you like to belong to the Quakers' meeting
> Yea friend yea.
> Then twiddle thy thumbs and follow me.

Each child goes behind the player in front till a long train is formed, they then kneel down all facing one way as close together as possible. A player at the back then gives a shove to the end of the line and all tumble over like nine-pins.

Emma Thoyts (Old Berkshire School Games, c. 1890)

SANFOIN

In the farmyard, halfway up the hill by the roadside, the engine and machine are standing between the sheds engaged in threshing out sanfoin from the rick. The farmer and his men are working the machine, and a crowd of children, small boys and girls, home from school, smothered with dust and grass seeds, their hair full of white particles, and their faces grimy with smoke and dust from the engine fires, are helping, or hindering, carrying away the chaff and chaving, in baskets, and by lapfuls. An elevator is attached to the rear part of the thresher; as the sanfoin leaves the drum it is shaken out into the box of this and raised high on to the rick. The engine is a small light portable, of 5 h.p., with tall chimney and bonnet on the top to prevent the sparks from flying out; the words 'PRIZE THRASHER' are painted, in large letters, all along the end of the machine nearest the engine. The tackle is the property of the farmer, and is worked by the regular farm staff, who get extra money for 'dreshin', however; when this is at an end, they stow the engine and machine in the big shed, and go on ploughing and drilling.

Not many farmers harvest sanfoin for seed. Where they do so, they watch the crop in the summer, and apportion off the best lot, to save for the autumn. When this is well ripe and dry, they cut it and stack it, and, after allowing it to stand a little while, thresh it out. In about five minutes the sack will be full of the seed, which rains down from the fans at a quick rate, though more slowly than wheat and barley. Oats fall most quickly from the thresher; with an extra good crop, a sackful of these will be run out in the space of a minute. A hundred-weight of sanfoin is counted a sack, and is valued at 30s. Only one sack receives the sanfoin as it falls; the others catch the

LOCKINGE

husks and grass seeds, which are called 'lops,' and which are promptly burned up out of the way. The word 'sanfoin' is seldom correctly articulated by the carters and rustics; they call it by a multitude of names, such as sankfoy, sinkfy, senkfay, sinfy, senfine, sanfin, sinfin, and so on.

Though the farmer works with his men all day on the ricks, they take but very little notice of his presence, and jog along at a comfortable rate, chatting to each other, and gossiping about the everyday affairs of the village. The hours of work are from 7 a.m. till 5 p.m., with an hour out for dinner, and generally a short spell in the morning and afternoon. The time soon slips by out in the open with the downs and valley in view, and there is a lack of that high tension which is so distressful a feature of the manufactory. It is not unusual, indeed, for the farmer and his men to disagree, and I have known them even to indulge in a hand-to-hand fight, and go on working as though nothing had happened; but there is never the dreadful hatred and long-pent-up smouldering passion about the farms as there is in the factory sheds; it is altogether unnatural and dehumanizing there. If the rustic has troubles, domestic or otherwise, he usually unburdens himself to the farmer and his wife, and obtains their sympathy, and is happy in their friendship; but in the factories this is impossible; a man cannot even

make a confidant of his nearest workmate; everyone there is too much concerned with himself to trouble about other people.

Alfred Williams

A LONGCOT GARDEN

A dear old woman in a lilac sunbonnet, whose husband, judging by his name, was probably a scion of a once powerful family in that part of the country, was digging in her garden. I made a remark to her as I passed, and she smiled so pleasantly that I stayed to talk, resting my elbow on the little wooden gate. She was only digging for pleasure, she assured me, when I apologised presently for hindering her work. And a pleasure indeed it must be, when you are nearly eighty, to be able to dig as she was digging on that sunny spring day with such vigour and energy. The little flower-bed that bordered the path from the gate to the cottage door was full of clumps of sweet blue violets and half-opened spring flowers. Wouldn't I like to come in and pick some? she asked, an invitation I lost no time in accepting.

90

WEST ILSLEY

She was proud of her garden, her own cabbage-patch, with the pride of possession which is so strong in the breasts of most English men and women. The feeling is completely bound up with English life, but it is by no means universally shared by the people of other nations. Not long ago in Norway I was noticing the almost general absence of gardens surrounding the houses. The want of them was rather striking, and I mused about it, wondering what was its probable cause. After all, I came to the conclusion it was sufficiently obvious: the soil is hard and unkind, and the difficulty in its cultivation so extreme that the Norwegian had either long ago given it up in despair, or instinct had taught him the futility of attempting it. Later I happened to speak on the subject to a native, a man who belonged to the labouring class, was a sea pilot, and had piloted Queen Victoria through the Fjords. In connection with this employment he had visited England and could speak English, hence the possibility of my carrying on a conversation with him. He quickly scattered to the winds the obvious conclusion I had come to. His reason for the absence of gardens, far from being an obvious one, was altogether unexpected, so difficult is it for the people of one nation to absolutely realise the sentiments and feelings of those of another, so rarely is the point of view quite the same.

'What did people want gardens for,' said the Norwegian, 'when they had the country before their eyes, and all the flowers upon the mountains and in the fields?' He could understand if one lived in the suburbs of London and had a little garden that one would value and treasure it, but in the country it seemed to be altogether a superfluity. The idea is interesting and somewhat poetical, but as the thoughts and ideas of a people must be in a great measure the result of their environment, perhaps this individual appropriation by the Norwegian of all the beauties of Nature lying spread before his eyes, the making them his own, as it were, by virtue of the sense of sight, may have been bred in him by the very fact which I alluded to – the arduous labour that the cultivation of a garden of his very own would entail.

And all the time, while she used her fork at intervals, and I was gathering for myself a bunch of her delicious violets, my old friend in her little English garden was chatting pleasantly. She talked of Madame Hughes at Uffington and Mr Thomas Hughes, who was known as Tom Brown. She had his books, 'a tract sort of copy'; her husband read to her from the *Scouring of the White Horse* in the evening. For generations her people had belonged to Longcot; she had got her schooling in the little school near the church. There, in one of the two rooms of

FORBURY PARK, READING

a tiny creeper-grown cottage, occupied now by the clerk, a Mrs Partridge kept school and taught the village girls to read and write, and sew, and mark samplers. And pleasant it must have been for the scholars in that little room, with the door leading right into the rose-covered porch, the lattice window opening into the garden, and the rooks cawing in the church-yard elms close by. In winter their lot was not so happy, for being warm went by favour. Truly shocking bribery and cor-ruption went on under the innocent-looking thatched roof of that little school. The scholars were supposed to bring contri-butions towards the upkeep of the school fire, and only those fortunate ones who were able to beg, borrow, or steal a stick, or a knob of coal, which they used to carry wrapped up in a piece of newspaper, were allowed to sit near the fire. The rest, with blue fingers and red noses, for the room was probably draughty, shivered outside. Children are thoughtless beings, and a dozen of them sitting round the fireplace would certain-ly effectually keep away even a sight of the grateful glow from those outside the circle.

Whether the same unrighteous system was practised by the boys' pedagogue I cannot say. Their school was just opposite,

tucked into a corner of the churchyard, and actually within its walls. A queer little place it must have been: a brick building about eighteen feet square. It looks like a tool-house or a stable; now the church coal is kept there. Upon a board over the door is painted a text which the rain and sun of many years have done their best to obliterate. And so well have they succeeded that only with careful scrutiny, and the judicious addition of a word here and there, is it possible to make out that it is a text at all. 'And they that be wise shall shine as the brightness of the fir-mament; and they that turn many to righteousness as the stars for ever and ever.' The queer, unpretentious little place seems so out of keeping with the grandeur of the beautiful words. Yet, after all, why? For the wisdom spoken of by the prophet is not the wisdom of book-learning, nor does the acquiring of it by the scholars depend upon the size in cubic inches of their school. And somehow I think that old woman in the lilac sun-bonnet, who was digging in her garden, had learnt it.

The writer of the following letter to a local out fitter neither joined the magic circle by the fire in the creeper-cov-ered cottage nor shivered miserably outside it. She probably did her lessons comfortably in the even temperature of the

92

BANK HOLIDAY PICNIC, UFFINGTON CASTLE

new red-brick parish school. Mrs Partridge must have died long before she was born; the old dame could not have been responsible for her education; and, after all, perhaps her scholars would have done as well:

'I arse please Mister Godding Will you please send 2 sut of dark Cloes for my to Bouys one six and one 14 please Mister Will you send it By Mister Bucher Will you send it as Dark as you Can dear sar me Wod not trouble you only their onkle just ded me Will pay you plese let me have it on Sataday for Sunday plese send 2 caps.'

The spelling may leave much to be desired, but the meaning is at any rate clear.

L.S.

THE WHITE HORSE

When you leave the train at Uffington you are in the heart of the Vale and the country of Tom Brown. [Thomas Hughes, author of *Tom Brown's Schooldays*, lived at Uffington.] It was at this little station that Dick alighted when he went to stay with his friend Joe, and his sweet sister Lucy, who had never been out of Berkshire in her life; who would sit in the evening stitching at a patchwork coverlet, fitting in all sorts of scraps of silk in the prettiest patterns in the world, while Dick talked in a low voice, in order not to disturb the old lady sleeping in her chair, about London and how people lived there and what they thought, falling in love with sweet Lucy while he did so.

Right up behind the station is the 'Swan', the little red-brick inn where Joe put up the pony when he and Dick made their famous expedition to White Horse Hill. And, very soon, a little further along the road, you can see the hill for yourself. 'There it stands, right up above all the rest, 900 feet above the sea, and the boldest, bravest shape for a chalk hill that you ever saw.' Thus enthusiastically breaks out Mr Hughes in praise of his beloved bit of country. Some authorities have tried to cast doubt upon the fact that the Horse being a memorial of Saxon victory; Mr Hughes will have none of it. 'When antiquarians differ,' he says, 'the tradition of the countryside may always be pretty safely believed. For the country people hold to such stories and hand them down.' Fain would one feel that he is right. When I first came within sight of that hill after leaving Uffington, I said to myself, 'Of course he is; he must and shall be.' Half the romance of the country would vanish into thin air if the White Horse were not carved by the Saxons after the great battle of Ashdown, where the good King Alfred made a final and splendid effort, where the Danes were routed, and peace and freedom once more assured.

One may differ, it is true, from the old chronicler in thinking that the figure of the animal is described in so masterly a manner that it may defy the painter's skill to give a more exact description. He also was enthusiastic to the point of exaggeration.

SCHOOLBOY GARDENERS, UFFINGTON

Nevertheless, it is a wonderful piece of work, and considering the size of the horse – it covers an acre of ground – the proportions are rather marvellous. The head had suffered and wanted reparation; the extremities of the hinder legs, from their unavoidable situation, the old chronicler goes on to say in his quaint way, when he saw the horse, had by the fall of rains been filled up in some measure with the washings from the upper part, so that in the nearest view of him, the tail, which had not suffered the same inconvenience and had continued entire from the beginning, seemed longer than the legs. Seeds of grass and plants fall into the trench which forms the animal, and growing up, obscure its shape. So it is necessary from time to time to clean it out. The operation is now performed in a very prosaic manner. But in olden times the scouring of the White Horse was the opportunity for feasting and merriment, with sports and all kinds of games. These scourings took place about every five years, but after 1825 there was an interval until 1838. Then the ancient custom was once more revived through the efforts of Lord Craven. The *Reading Mercury* of that time comments on the auspicious time chosen for this revival, the period of a double event, in which our youthful and beloved Queen first wore the British crown, and in which an heir was born to the ancient and noble house of Craven.

At the scouring of the 1843, Simon Stone, the far-famed Somersetshire backsword champion, was present

and all the old-fashioned games took place. By 1857 the scouring had assumed a comparatively modern character. Wombwell's menagerie travelled down to Berkshire for the event. And a tremendous struggle there was to get the caravan up the hill; it stuck fast four or five times, in spite of the efforts of twenty-four horses to get it along. The marvel is, not that it stuck half-way, but that it ever reached the top at all.

We are apt to smile sometimes at the ingenuity and inventive powers of the modern advertiser, and his avidity to seize upon any passing occurence or fact that will serve his purpose. But can the ingenuity of any modern advertiser beat that of a Vale tradesman who seventy years ago applied that Saxon victory to an advertisement of his home-made ketchup?

> 'Deer is the vendor's native town
> (Though cheap the product of his skill),
> There Alfred battled for his Crown,
> And graved the White Horse on our Hill
> Our Hill of picnic spots the chief,
> Where fair ones couched on flowery moss
> Enjoy our matchless Vale-fed beef,
> Married to Goodman's matchless Sauce.'

L.S.

94

WINDSOR

LETTERS FROM COURT

Windsor Castle, November 20th 1895
We had a most interesting ceremony this afternoon, i.e. the reception of the African Chiefs and I was present with the Queen as well as the Lady-in-Waiting, the first time I have ever had such an honour. To begin the story we had a State Lunch, the Gentlemen in levée dress and I had Lord Selborne on my right and Chief Bathoeu on my left; he seemed the least attractive of the blacks but enjoyed his food thoroughly and ate in a very civilised manner. Indeed their manners were excellent quite a lesson to many Britons! They are all tee-totallers and drink nothing but lemonade but Khama is the finest of them and wins golden opinions wherever he goes. Lord Selborne says he is a better Christian than anyone he knows and a very intelligent man to boot, a great hero. I must say he looks it and I was so struck with his face and slim upright figure. The Queen received the Chiefs in the White Drawing Room seated on a Throne like a chair, and the Chiefs advanced through a long line of Life Guards with drawn swords, stationed in the two large Drawing Rooms. The Queen welcomed them and they presented their gifts, three Karosses or rugs of leopard skins of doubtful smell but intrinsic worth. Then the Queen spoke saying she was glad to have them under her rule and protection and felt very strongly the necessity of preventing strong drink from entering their lands. This was duly interpreted and they replied each in turn. Then the Queen gave them a New Testament in their tongue with her own hands and huge framed photos, and an Indian

PRINCESS ALICE OF ALBANY, WINDSOR

SIX CLERICS AT WANTAGE

Shawl was handed to each of them by Lord Clarendon, and with grateful grunts they retired backwards leaving us much impressed by their quiet dignity and wonderful self-possession. I could see they were immensely impressed but they tried not to show their feelings and succeeded admirably.

Windsor Castle, November 26th 1895

Francis will have told you of Victor's angelic behaviour, he kissed the Queen's hand twice in the most courtier-like manner and answered all her questions quite promptly telling Her Majesty you were at your office and that you rode a 'flying machine'. The Queen said, 'I suppose you mean a bicycle, dear', upon which he answered in shrill tones, 'Nanny says it is a flying machine' which made her laugh heartily. Then Her Majesty said, 'Do you know who I am?' 'Keenie' replied he quite loud and decided. The Queen thought him prettier than ever and more like me and admired his white satin frock so much. So did the dear Duchess of Albany who came to my room to play with him for over twenty minutes. The Royal Nurses gave a glowing account of his manners to Princess Beatrice so I think we may surely congratulate ourselves upon his bringing-up as far as it goes.

Windsor Castle, December 7th 1897

The Queen was very amusing yesterday about games at Public Schools, football she thinks very barbarous, cricket would not be so bad if the ball were softer. I was appealed to as to whether it could not be made of some kind of composition.

I stood up for athletics but granted Rugby football was a desperate game. At dinner we had much talk (a 'hen' party) about music and musicians, the Queen as usual inveighed against Oratorios and said she could not forget the boredom of *The Messiah* heard in York Minster when she was about 16. I could not agree about this and praised Handel and the whole tribe of oratorio writers, so you see I was in opposition all day long!

Marie Mallet

WINDSOR DIARY 1900

November 29

Twelve months ago today I rose at 5a.m. to see a squadron of 1st Life Guards pass this house on the way to South Africa to take part in the war. Today such of them as have passed safely through the ordeal, returned to the barracks, having landed at Southampton this morning. An enormous crowd had assembled and loudly cheered the men. Previously to going to Barracks they went to the Castle to be inspected by the Queen. The men were on foot, as *only one* of the beautiful creatures they rode a year ago has survived. This one was led up behind the men and was an object of pathetic interest. It is said its master was one of the first to be killed in battle. It looked as if most of its spirit had gone out of it. The men

RAILWAY STATION, LAMBOURNE

made no pretence at marching, but straggled up the hill and down Peascod St. anyhow, many having friends clinging to them. They had, however, to keep up a pretty good pace as the brass bands of both the Life Guards and Foot Guards led the way, followed by about 20 men of their own regiment who had met them on horseback acted as rear-guard. The men, for the most part, were looking very serious and far from in good condition.

November 30

About a month ago Lord Wolsely, Commander-in-Chief of the Queen's Forces, and Lord Roberts, Commander-in-Chief of the Forces in South Africa, issued separate appeals to the English people to abstain from treating the men returning from active service with intoxicating drink. Tonight the men who returned yesterday to Windsor, have been entertained by the town authorities at the White Hart Hotel and I have just seen them return to barracks, many of them in a most disgraceful condition, staggering and stupid. How it has come about with a mayor who is a Total Abstrainer I have yet to learn. There was a committee appointed, I believe by the town Council, to make and carry out the arrangements, and probably they have overruled the mayor and made the men drunk.

Alexander Elliot

LAMBOURNE

The stranger who chances to enter Lambourne, the little town at the terminus of the railway, for the first time from the sta-

tion will certainly experience pangs of disappointment and apprehension. Lambourne is being rapidly built over. Hideous erections – you know the kind; they always make their appearance when the building fiend pounces down upon a place; red houses pointed with white stretching out in long lines – meet the eye. Really for the moment they cause one bitterly to regret the railway, the natural cause of the disfigurement. Presently, however, you feel better. As you go farther into the village – town, the little place can really hardly be called – thatched houses and nice old buildings meet your eye once more: houses that in spite of the condemnation of the reformer, and even that of the sanitary inspector, you feel certain must be better to live in than those ugly jerry-built, and certainly draughty, little modern abodes. I do not deny that the interiors of the picturesque houses are capable of improvement; indeed, in many cases they cry out loudly for it. But the walls are thick, and the thatch is cosy and comfortable, they have an individuality – and ugh! those red and white boxes, they are all built exactly alike. You would hear your neighbours' quarrels through the walls.

Could anything be more solid and comfortable, and delightfully picturesque as well, than those old almshouses near the church at Lambourne? It would be quite worth while being an old person for the sake of living in them, though I am bound in confidence to say that even in old age I think it just possible after a time that the life might pall. But they are peaceful abodes. Over a gateway an inscription informs us that they were built by John Eastbury, A.D. 1507. Good old John Eastbury, one feels quite grateful to his memory, as one enters under the archway, even for the sight of such picturesque peacefulness. Grateful also one is to Henry Hippesley when he restored them for not having departed one atom from the

LIFE GUARDS, GEORGE HOTEL, LAMBOURNE

original design. In the middle of the little courtyard stands a grand old wooden pump; there is – comforting thought – plenty of water for drinking and washing. The houses are built upon three sides of a square, surrounded by a narrow cloister. Here, under shelter, the old people can take a constitutional in comfort when it rains, or pop in and out of each other's houses for a gossip without wetting their feet. And the worm-eaten wood of that cloister is of such a deep tone – black with age. The mass of glowing flowers – crimson hollyhocks, scarlet geraniums, and purple clematis – gain largely in brilliancy of effect with the dark wood of the cloister as a background.

All the attractions of the place seem to be concentrated round the church. Besides the almshouses, there is the beautiful old cross, with the Elizabethan manor house close by.

L.S.

SHEPHERDS

The shepherd had his sport in former days in catching wheatears with springs set in the turf, and often made a good profit in selling them to poulterers in Brighton; but these birds have diminished greatly in numbers in modern times, and the sport is, I believe, abandoned. Moreover, he made a little profit by collecting plovers' eggs.

In these days the shepherd's domain is decreased by the advent of the plough and the building of houses; so that his importance and independence are somewhat diminished. But he is not dead yet – far from it – and you may still see him on the Downs with his dog, minding his sheep as his forefathers did a thousand years ago.

To those of us who visit him in his solitude he appears to be a very lonesome person, one to be greatly pitied; but he is never distressed by his solitary state. On the Berkshire Downs a doctor was riding, and meeting a shepherd asked where he lived. The shepherd pointed to a solitary cottage where he, his wife, and bairns dwelt.

'What a lonely place to live in!' replied the doctor. 'However do you manage when you are ill? Where can you get a doctor to attend you?'

'Doctor! We do'ent want no doctors. We allays dies a natural death!'

On the same Downs a canvasser for the election of a county councillor was beating up the rustic voters, and shouted to our solitary keeper of the sheep:

'Vote for Mr Smith, the people's friend!'

'Voate!' replied the shepherd. 'What's a voate?'

'Are you so stupid that you do not know what a vote means? Don't you take any interest in politics?'

'Tics! Now I knows what you be talking about. Tics! Yon sheep be full on 'em; but I never 'eard o' them polions before.'

ANNUAL WALKING RACE, NEWBURY

It must not be supposed that the shepherd was entirely ignorant of votes and politics. Like most rustics he is always on his guard when strangers ask him questions, and pretends to be quite stupid in order not to incriminate himself, to save himself trouble, and to defeat the 'foreigner'.

Peter Ditchfield

A LOYAL SHEPHERD

For many years the Rectory of Childrey was most comfortably endowed, for the rent of the farm was once as much as £1,000 a year. Think of that when Income Tax was in pence! But those times had long passed when my father was appointed to Childrey. Still, the farm was a good one and the rent considerable, and if the tenant had done his share things might have gone pretty well. Unfortunately he drank too much and idled steadily, leaving his foreman, Shepherd Elliot, to try in vain to be foreman and shepherd and farmer at the same time. Elliot was the most interesting man that I ever met among agricultural labourers, for besides being very knowledgeable he possessed the faculty, rare among rural folk, of being able to tell what he knew. Generally one found the Berkshire labourers rather inarticulate, except, perhaps, when they told of

NEWBURY

99

CROQUET AT SULHAM

olden times. Elliot was full of knowledge about the wild life of the country, the hares and their habits, the partridges, the 'rook-hawks', as he called peregrine falcons, the deposit of mist and dew in the dew ponds on the Downs, and, above all, of his sheep. His description of the rising of water in the dew ponds was terse and clear. 'These vappers draw up out of the ground', he said; I used to think of dew as falling, but Elliot went further back to when the moisture rose from the land. 'Then when they make a mist it draws towards the pond and the water from them settles in it.' 'Elliot, you seem to know so many things.' 'Yes, sir,' he replied, 'I speriences.' To observe, to remember, to ponder and discover the reason why, Elliot compressed into the words 'I sperience'. A humble student of nature myself, I found that he had shown me the right way to go to work.

It was beautiful to see him with his flock, especially at lambing time, and to note how he knew every one of his three hundred ewes individually. Once one of our pupils, looking at many lambs running with the ewes, said to him: 'How do they know which is their mother?' Elliot looked puzzled and answered, 'But would not you know your mother?' Sometimes when the sheep were penned in hurdles for the night not far from his house something would alarm them, perhaps a fox prowling round the fold, and they would begin to rush about. Several of them carried bells, and of better tone than the ordinary rough sheep bell, and their sound gave Elliot warning. Again I quote his words: 'When I hear the bells, then I calls to they, and directly they hears my voice they is still.' He had beautiful blue eyes, well-formed features, and his

ROBERT LAW AND MARY ELLEN, COLD ASH

DAPHNE AND HARRY MANSELL PLYDELL, THORPE LEA HOUSE, WINDSOR

whole aspect showed character and ability. Perhaps the finest proof of his character was that only once did I hear him say a word against his employer, bitterly though it grieved him to see the farm going to ruin. His complaint was that 'The Bear, that do have had so many quarters of oats for drink'. The Bear Hotel was his employer's favourite house. But at last Elliot could no longer save the farmer from bankruptcy, and then he was at once taken on as shepherd by a far better employer.

James Cornish

PAPER CHASE

Up to this term no paper chase had been held here for more than two years, but arrangements were made for one on October 21st. The novelty of the affair and the fact that a half holiday was given expressly for the purpose, induced nearly the whole School to turn out for it.

At a meeting held on the previous day, Morland, Townsend and Russwurm, were elected to run as hares. Accordingly the three named started off soon after 2 p.m., and were followed by the junior division of the hounds after an interval of ten minutes, the senior division starting a few minutes later. The track was first laid at the bottom of the School Lane, and proceeding down Box Hall after a mile or so of fields, came out on the Oxford road at Northcote. About half an hour after the start and close to Radley Wood, the hares were caught. Mr Paul, closely followed by Bennetts and Holmes, being the first up.

After a rest of a minute or two, Mr Paul kindly consented to run with the hares and lay a track, and the same hares again started off. By this time most of the rear guard had come up, and after giving the hares about twelve minutes law, the hounds started off in pursuit; the course being laid through Radley Woods.

After leaving these Townsend was quickly run down; Bennetts, who ran well throughout, again being first up. The other two hares however, kept up better than before, though Morland was eventually caught when close to Radley Station, he having had to stop owing to cramp.

By this time the paper had come to an end, and all took the nearest way home. Russwurm remained uncaught to the end, and with practice and judgment would make a good cross country runner.

ABINGDON

The first of the hounds to arrive were Bennetts, Shopland, and the two Holmes,' who all came in about 5.15, all the four having run especially well.

On the whole the course was rather different to what the School has been accustomed to in previous years, there being less jumps and ditches than usual; but the thick underwood in the Radley Woods caused several fellows to come to grief. In future it is to be hoped that the time of starting and arriving home will be 'clocked,' as then the various running powers of the fellows could be gauged more accurately.

Everyone was glad to see the Head Master turn out, and very useful he was to some of the younger boys at a difficult hedge. And so ended a very pleasant run.

The Abingdonian [Abingdon School Magazine] 1890

TROUBLES IN SUNNINGDALE PARISH

Many of the well-to-do people in the parish were most kind in giving me generous help for the Sick and Needy Fund, and with the assistance of good district visitors we could help many cases, especially the children. If one of them needed attention I could be sure of letters to hospitals in London, Reading or Windsor, and this was especially useful when the eyes of children or of their mothers needed attention. Over and over again our doctor would find a mother suffering from headaches and send her to me, so that I could arrange a visit to Reading and pay for glasses. There was nothing in my pastoral life I liked better than fussing about for men, women and children who needed care. Often they, especially the men, were anything but ready to be 'taken care of', and sometimes would flatly refuse to have spectacles for their girls.

There were about two thousand people in the parish, and their names and faces were rather more than my curate and I could remember, but by frequent visits to the schools it was possible to know all, or nearly all, the children.

This was before the days of Unemployment Insurance, and as a parish Parson my anxieties and difficulties were many during those years. There came a trouble which was really terrible – diphtheria in the schools; not many cases, but perhaps one among the Infants and another in the Upper School. Then the Schools had to be closed, the rooms disinfected, and the children isolated. There was no isolation hospital, so they had to be nursed at home. Also there was no drainage system and the cottage gardens were foul. For weeks no new cases would occur and then came another outbreak, generally among the children. The Ecclesiastical Parish lay in three Rural Districts – Egham, Chertsey, and Old Windsor, with the latter controlling by far the greater area.

SILVER STREET, READING

OLD ANGEL INN, THEALE

ALBERT LAUNDRY, WINDSOR

I began to agitate for a drainage scheme, but this was opposed by Ascot, Sunninghill, and most of the inhabitants of Sunningdale, for it would be costly. In the second and third of our visitations of diphtheria fatal cases occurred, and among them two dear little boys who were much loved. This made me so grieved and so angry that I lost patience and spoke and wrote rather bitterly. But there were excuses. I had urged the Chertsey Council to amend the insanitary conditions of Brownhall. One of the Councillors asked who I was, and on hearing that I was Vicar of the parish, said: 'Why does he not look after people's *souls?*' In the Egham part, several children in one family went down with diphtheria, and as the mother was expecting a baby the Guardians moved them to another cottage close by where father, mother and two children recovered and the mother came safely through her confinement, but it was a callous action.

There were wise and kind people in Sunningdale who helped me and encouraged me to persevere, and gradually the opposition became weaker and the support for the drainage scheme stronger, till at last a postcard vote was taken; the majority were in favour, and the Council were at length able to launch the scheme which they had planned long before.

James Cornish

OLD BETTY HICKS

Here and there, lying at the side of and in between the woods are patches and stretches of common land, which strike one as being ideal places for gipsies; and the gipsies have recognized the fitness also. There is a Romany settlement (these people resent the sobriquet of gipsy) between Brimpton and Aldermaston towards Tadley. At all the feasts and village fairs of the surrounding country there is no more familiar figure than old Betty Hicks, who belongs to this particular settlement; no more familiar and no more quaint one than Betty in her little donkey-cart, a black silk hood bonnet on her head and a short clay pipe in her mouth. Betty is a hawker, or 'travelling lady,' as she is designated by her people. But travelling days for her are nearly over; both she and the old donkey have pretty nearly come to the end of their tether. The time cannot be so very far ahead when the fairs and the feasts and the roads of South Berkshire will see her well-known figure no more.

Betty is a 'character.' There are stories told of her drinking propensities. She has often been seen, it is said, lying at the bottom of her little cart, while the old donkey, unguided, makes its way slowly and carefully homewards. Perhaps Betty owes her life to her donkey. For who knows – the stories told about her may be true; perhaps she does drink. She smokes unlimited tobacco and, according to the opinion of one of her

READING NATURAL HISTORY SOCIETY, BUCKLEBURY

old neighbours, 'it isn't the wittels wot kips Betty going, but the 'baccy and the little drap o' drink.'

Betty shares with all the people of gipsy blood their extreme reverence for the dead. After her daughter's death, having nursed her devotedly during her last illness, the old mother walked a distance of nearly three miles with the aid of two sticks over frozen ground – it was too slippery to take the donkey – to visit the grave. 'There was father, mother, brothers, sisters, and children all lying in the graveyard,' she said, with infinite pathos, 'and when I got there I don't know how I felt.'

Within the memory of the older inhabitants, the people of the settlement to which Betty belongs have lived in tents; then they took to vans; now they reside mostly in houses which they have built themselves, having made a piece of common land their own by buying it, or squatting. Some of the tribe still prefer their vans; these are chiefly those who have kept much to their ancient traditions, and are more exclusive. They all preserve still their own language, though now the children go to the village schools many of their words have become known. But the Romanies will never lose their secretiveness. Persuasion causes them to disclose very little; but mystery shrouding them will never be wholly torn away.

L.S.

HOOP-CUTTING

Every nine years in Berkshire the copses are cut down. This cutting begins in the winter and goes on into early spring. Gradually, instead of the red-brown haze upon some hill or rising ground, an empty space appears, and we feel some of that inevitable sadness that always comes with the felling of trees. It may be some beauty of the country which before was hidden is now opened out, some distant range of hills that we had not seen – perhaps we can even get a better sight of the sunset. We are not reconciled. We miss the soft green curtain that we have watched being hung out there year after year – ever since we can remember, it would almost seem, for nine years is a long period in any life.

When the time has come for a wood to be cut down, it is sold as it stands to a man who is called a copse-dealer. He undertakes the whole work, and hires the labour. It is for him that the copsemen and hoopmen work. The copsemen are the first to begin; they are the men who cut down the wood, after it has been divided into lots or 'drifts' of five acres to each copse-man. They not only cut the trees, but trim them, and make the wood up into bundles to be sold either for firewood or broom-making, and prepare the rest for the hoopmen to work upon.

HOOP MAKING IN A BERSHIRE WOOD

And when one talks about the 'hoops,' it is necessary to explain, for though they are called hoops, and will be hoops in another stage of their existence, they are certainly not hoops in the general acceptation of the word when they leave the copse. Then they are only straight pieces of wood, which presently will be bent into hoops round tubs and barrels, and used to strengthen and bind together boxes and casks. Most of the hoopmen have been at their work all their lives. It looks simple enough – but is it? A closer inspection will show you that it is not so easy as it appears. One old hoopman has been at it for fifty years, and his three sons now work under him. He is quite ready to be communicative and to explain the intricacies of what has become to him an absolutely mechanical performance. Though he cannot be said to be a very lucid exponent of it, he at least makes you understand, which is something. He is a little old man, whose back is bent with ceaseless stooping at his work. He wears a leathern apron, and leathern sleeves over his coat. He suffers from 'rheumatics,' and acknowledges quite gravely to carrying a piece of alum in his pocket for the complaint. The remedy does not seem to have been a very efficacious one; perhaps his faith in it has not been sufficient.

Upon a day, of which the old man remarks that 'it couldn't have bin better if we'd med it oursels,' it is pleasant to go into the copse and watch the men at their work. The sun shines warmly, there is almost a throb of spring in the air, one can almost fancy a faint greenness in the trees; but the cuckoo has not come yet, and March has to be got through. It will be well to make the most of the day, the warmth, and the sun; on the morrow there may be frost, perhaps even snow.

The copse is not all felled yet. Upon two sides of the bare space which has been already cleared a red-brown mass of trees still stands – oaks, and ashes, and alders, with here and there the slim stem of a silver birch; the last will be left there when its humbler companions have been laid low. The copse-men are at work with their bill-hooks, cutting and trimming, and making the wood into bundles. Gradually the space grows. It is covered with the bronze leaves of the year before, out of which project the naked stumps of the trees that have been already cut. Presently they will be hidden by the bluebells. In the centre, in the clearing, surrounded by great heaps of cream-coloured shavings, and the white bundles of finished hoops, the old man stands, patiently measuring and splitting the pieces of wood, as he has done for more than fifty years; and his sons at some little distance off are 'sheeving' and finishing them. The arrangement for measuring the wood is primitive enough, yet it might be difficult to contrive a more modern method to answer the purpose better. At regular intervals from each other and the stake upon which the hoops are cut and split, posts are driven into the ground, so that they

106

THE GREYHOUND, BESSELSLEIGH

just project above it. One end of the piece of wood to be measured is laid against one of the posts, and the other against the stake, and the post which the end of the 'hoop' reaches determines its length. The end that is upon the stake is then chopped to make the length exactly right, and with the same tool, a sharp little axe, the piece of wood is split through the middle. It is then thrown upon the proper pile of hoops, and is ready to be planed or shaved. Does it all sound very complicated? – well that, perhaps, is the result of its simplicity.

And then comes the 'sheeving,' which is accomplished by another simple but effectual contrivance, called a 'brake,' which is set up by the men themselves in this way: A thick piece of timber, which works upon a pivot, is fastened to three uprights, and weighted at one end with a heavy bundle of faggots, or a block of wood, tied to it by a rope. Crossing this movable piece of wood at the top is a round roll of irons about a foot in length. The movable piece of wood is worked by the knee being placed against it, the pressure either releasing or holding fast the 'hoop' when the end of it is placed under the parallel rod of iron. Whilst it is thus held fast it is quickly sliced thin and smooth, or 'sheeved,' with a very sharp knife having a handle at both ends.

At last the 'hoops' are finished and ready for the market. The bundles are made up with their shaved or white side out-

wards and are bound very neatly and tightly together. In the distance, when they have lately been out, before the weather has touched them, they gleam like bundles of ivory. In the spring, for a long time, upon the roads and in the lanes, carts with loads of white bundles may be seen. They are on their way to the wharf, where the bundles will be put on the barges to float slowly towards their destination, which is finally London, upon the bosom of the canal.

L.S.

WHITE HORSE INN

The old White Horse Inn stands in the centre of the village, at an angle of the road, a short way down from the hill. The building is of the fifteenth or sixteenth century, rambling in structure, with flattish roof, large bay windows fitted with quaint panes of glass, and spacious rooms within, which have sheltered many a weary traveller from the bitter blasts that rage along the hill and over the graven figure of the Horse in the solitary winter nights. Around the entrance are piled up large sarsen-stones, gathered about the high downs, and each with an history, which seem to emphasize the great age of the inn;

BISCUIT PACKING AT HUNTLEY AND PALMERS, READING

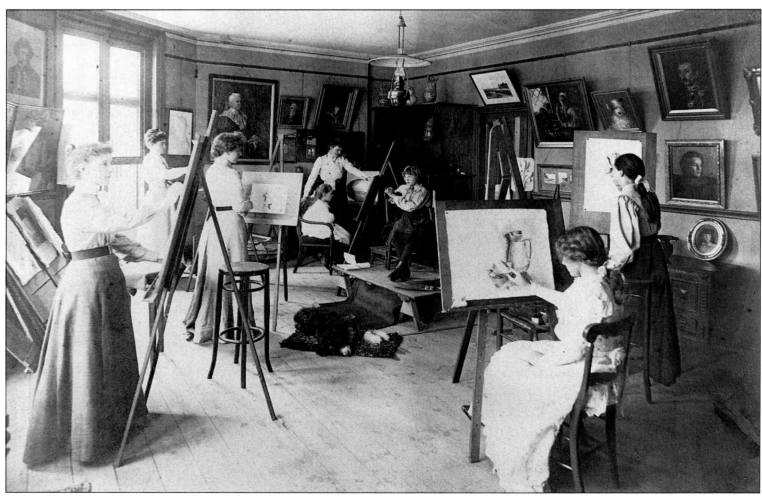

VALPY STREET SCHOOL OF ART, READING

WARGRAVE

while inside are to be seen the antique oak panelling, old-fashioned settees, and a splendid speciment of the ancient 'ingle nook' – a survival of other days – around which the old folks sat and drank from the loving cup, toasting each other in the ruddy firelight, and telling tales of adventures on the downs with robbers, poachers, and sheep-stealers, with which the region of the White Horse was formerly infested. All that is at an end now, though there is no lack of tourists and visitors at the inn, who come to walk upon the steep hill, or view the White Horse, and lounge on the worm-eaten settees, sipping ale or coffee, charmed with the pleasant air of antiquity that prevails about the place.

The names of the inns about the downs and valley are usually local in origin and relation: the references are easily understood, though here and there you meet with one that is more difficult of construction, which may be symbolical, as The Shears, or The Cross Keys . . . characteristic names of local inns are: The White Horse, The Black Horse, The Running Horse, The Shepherd's Rest, The Woodman, The True Heart, The Fox and Hounds, The Cow, The Elm Tree, The Plough, The Harrow, The Blue Lion, The Boar, and Trip the Daisy.

Small beer or 'swanky,' was sold at the cottages, in times past, at 1½d. a quart. Then tea was practically unknown to the labourers; they had ale for breakfast, dinner, and supper. The landlords of the village inns still keep the shoe-like tin

MORLAND'S BREWERY, ABINGDON

BRIDGE STREET, SONNING

WILLIAM LAILEY, BOWLMAKER OF BUCKLEBURY

vessels for warming the beers for their customers in the winter; these they thrust into the coals 'to take the jaa (jaw) off' – to remove the cold snack from the liquor – as they say.

Alfred Williams

THE BOWL MAKER

The march of the seasons upon Bucklebury Common is a procession of beauty. In the spring, when the birch-trees are coming into leaf, their young green stands out against a dark background of huge holly trees. The holly-trees are a great feature of Bucklebury Common. Presently, as far as the eye can reach, the gorse is yellow, and the heather flushes a warm pink under the summer sun. Later still there is golden bracken. Long trails of red climb over the bramble-bushes, and the leaves of the great trees rustle down and form a bronze-coloured carpet upon the pathways. Then comes the winter, and the common is silent in a solemn harmony of purple and brown and grey. The wind makes mournful music, and the heavy clouds pile themselves up over the desolate groups of fir-trees. Bucklebury Common is weirdly beautiful in winter.

In a specially wooded part, only to be found by those who know where to look for it, is a great pond. There you can sit for hours and hear no human sound. The cooing of the wood-pigeon or the cry of the dabchick, as it dives in and out among the water-weeds, or an occasional whirr of a pheasant close by may be heard. Nothing else breaks the

THE BELL, SHURLOCK ROW

quiet. All round the pond the trees bend over their own reflections until they sadly and silently efface them with their leaves.

Some parts of the common have been scenes of industry in past days; a remnant of this industry still remains. Hidden away in a corner, an interesting labour is still carried on, the finished specimens of which you are no doubt familiar with in the shop windows of Bond Street or Regent Street. I mean the wooden soap bowls; ordinary and common objects enough – you have never noticed them with any special interest. But after you have seen them made upon Bucklebury Common you will look at them with different eyes. They are made in all sizes: the smaller are used as cash bowls; some very large ones are in use at the Mint. Many of those in the shops, it is true, are now machine-made; this of necessity, because the people who can still make them by hand have mostly died out. Fifty or a hundred years ago there were numbers of families engaged in the bowl-cutting industry on the common, while now only one family is left in which the art has been preserved. None of the younger people learn; it seems such a pity. This family is justly proud of its bowl-cutting; it has been doing it for generations. The father of the old man who still works at it used to take his bowls by road all the way to London in his cart, starting before sunrise, and sleeping one night in the city. A terrible place he thought it, and glad enough he was to get back to Bucklebury.

POSTMAN DELIVERING SUTTON'S SEEDS FROM READING

111

THE 'HOLE IN THE WALL', PANGBOURNE

Linger for half an hour and ask leave to watch the work, it will well repay you. The bowls are cut out from a huge rough block of wood upon a home-made lathe – many of the tools also are of home manufacture. Here lies so much of the charm. The work is solid, good, and lasting, as only hand-made work can be.

L.S.

THE QUEEN VISITS MESSRS SUTTON AND SONS AT WINDSOR SHOW

Her Majesty the Queen, accompanied by the Prince of Wales and other members of the Royal family, visited the showyard again yesterday (Friday) morning, and, during their drive round the show, the Royal party stopped several minutes at Messrs Sutton and Sons' handsome range of offices to inspect some of the features of this interesting exhibit. Mr Martin J. Sutton, Mr A.W. Sutton, and Mr Leonard Sutton had the honour of receiving her Majesty, who was graciously pleased to express satisfaction with what she had seen, and thanked Mr M.J. Sutton for the beautiful floral decorations provided by his firm for the Royal pavilion. Mr Martin Sutton had the honour also of presenting her Majesty with photographs of the gardens of the Royal pavilion and a magnificently bound copy of the

'Sutton Album', as a *souvenir* of the exhibition; also a bouquet of splendid gloxinias, grown at Messrs Sutton's Reading seed gardens.

Berkshire Chronicle, 29 June 1889

THE RIVER AT PANGBOURNE

> O Pangbourne is pleasant in sweet Summertime,
> And Streatley and Goring are worthy of rhyme:
> The sunshine is hot and the breezes are still,
> The River runs swift under Basildon Hill!
> To lounge in a skiff is delightful to me,
> I'm feeling as lazy as lazy can be;
> I don't care to sail and I don't care to row –
> Since I'm lucky enough to be taken in tow!

Ashby-Sterry

OLD JOHN

Old John is a picturesque figure, in the brown corduroys that have taken the place, alas! of the smock frock. He wears a soft grey felt hat, turned up in front; below it is his long white

WOKINGHAM

hair. A merry twinkle animates his light blue eyes as he leans forward with both hands upon his stick. 'I recklet, I recklet,' he reiterates as preface to story following story. He has done many things in his time. In his day people did not mind making themselves generally useful, and thought no scorn to turn their hand to any work. He began when he was 'a little nipper' of seven, to earn his shilling a week by looking after horses, when he was so tiny that he had to climb into the manger to tie the animals up. So he has had only a fortnight's schooling in his life, but, as often happens, his natural shrewdness and observation have taught him a great deal, more perhaps than any book-learning ever would. Among his accomplishments was included that of being able to sow a field of ten acres with a gallon of 'turmut seed,' which, though it may be no proof of skill to your mind or to mine, to the initiated stands as a tremendous feat. 'They don't know how to sow nowadays – leastways, not with small grain; the larger is easier to manage.' His experience of life has not been confined altogether to Bucklebury; the old man has travelled. He has been to London several times, stayed for a month at a time, and thoroughly enjoyed it. He has visited the National Gallery (his daughter's husband being one of the officials). 'There *were* some picturs there,' he said, which simple comment, after all, shows an appreciation sadly lacking amongst many people boasting of education, judging by the remarks overheard occasionally in the galleries.

John and his wife are great herbalists, and supply a herb doctor in London with numerous medicinal plants. They rec-ommend tansy tea for rheumatism, marsh mallow poultices for wounds, and white lily root ointment for gatherings. But the herbs by which they set most store are wood sage and horehound. These are wonderful plants, capable apparently of curing almost every ill under the sun indiscriminately. Virtue undoubtedly there is in all these simple remedies. It is a pity that their value has been so much lost sight of.

More doubt may possibly be felt as to the efficacy of the treatment for warts suggested by the old couple. 'Werts' might be cured, they said, by cutting slits in a stick of alder, or by making holes according to their number in walnut leaves. The walnut leaves – and this is very important – must then be buried secretly or put down a well. As the leaves decay the warts will disappear.

L.S.

THE BARN DANCE

When any local or national festivity takes place a barn is swept, its usual contents are thrust out of sight, and the walls and wooden pillars supporting the roof are decorated with evergreens. At Whitsuntide, during the feast a rustic dance is held here, at which young and old foot it on the boarded floor. The music is supplied by native talent, and consists of a dulcimer, a concertina, and a flute or violin whose quaint tinkletankle adds to the archaic character of the proceeding. Youth

KINGSTON LISLE

NEWBURY

and age at such times appear to reverse their parts, for while the passing generation plunges recklessly 'down the middle and up again,' amid racy comment and jovial laughter, the children trip through the barn dance with a gravity that matches their grace, and young men and maidens perform the redowa together wearing an air of solemnity which would become a funeral. A certain rigorous etiquette prevails at these functions: it would be considered the height of impropriety for a girl to take her partner's arm, but the latter would be deemed singularly lacking in gallantry if he relinquished his clasp of her waist during a pause in the dance. A stranger from another sphere of life, having strayed into a gathering like that I am describing, transgressed this code of manners, and to his amazement found his conduct regarded as a deliberate insult and his arm indignantly refused by outraged modesty.

In some villages it is the custom to bring the feast week to a close by a second dance on the last evening: this, in local phraseology, is styled 'pinning up' the feast, and the process attracts many visitors from the surrounding villages. I have been often told that Mary or Em'ly Jane is gone to 'pin up the feast' at such and such a place; and much perplexed I was at first by this mysterious expression.

For a harvest supper, tables are set down the length of the barn and all the hands on the farm, together with their wives,

NEWBURY BOROUGH FIRE BRIGADE

are invited. The repast, in which beef and mutton, bread and cheese and beer, figure on an ample scale, is of course the main feature of the entertainment; when this important and lengthy business has been discussed, the lighter items on the programme follow. Pipes are lighted, glasses replenished, speeches and songs are delivered. I say 'delivered' advisedly in connection with the latter, which are, for the most part, ancient ditties, scarce fit for repetition here, treating of the follies and sorrows of too-confiding village maidens. They number from ten to a dozen verses, supplemented by a chorus in which the women join unabashed, and are trolled forth by the singer with a seriousness of demeanour suggestive of anything rather than mirth.

Eleanor Hayden

A BLEWBURY COTTAGE

In Blewbury one is always breaking the tenth commandment. It would be easy enough, I have not the slightest doubt, to break there each and every commandment contained in either or both of the Tables of the Law, had one a mind so to do; but the tenth commandment, as regards one item of it, your neighbour's house, it is absolutely impossible to keep. The outside of those picturesque Elizabethan cottages is temptation enough; the interiors of some of them make one feel quite sure that the tenth commandment was made on purpose to be broken – once, at any rate. Having accepted the courteous invitation to 'step in' that was given me by one kindly old lady, I gave expression to the feelings that were overcoming me. The day was hot, the roads extremely dusty, the glare of their white surface made my eyes ache, when suddenly I was

READING

ELISHA HICKS' ROSE NURSERY, TWYFORD

transported into the dim light of a cool room – marvellously cool, because of the creeper-covered windows, with low rafters and red-brick floor, an oak dresser covered with shining blue china, a grandfather clock and oak table. A sweet scent of flowers came in at the open door, and a soothing sound of bees from a swarm that had taken possession of the roof, just over the porch. And that modern longing which may be described as wanting to 'eat one's cake and have it,' in other words, to seize all the sweets and reject all the disagreeables, took possession of me. I thought what an ideal 'week-end' cottage this one would make, or little place to come down to in the summer, when one happened to be tired of the noise and bustle of London, and desired rest and quiet. And I put my thoughts into words: 'I *should* like to have a cottage like this.' The moment the words were uttered I saw they might well bear misinterpretation. That to the dear old lady who had lived in the cottage for so many years, not only in the glorious summer, when flowers were bright in the garden, when the sun shone and everything looked gay, but also in the dreary winter, when the snow lay heaped up round the doorway, when the evenings closed in early and the wind howled, and the rain beat up against the windows in the dark – to the dear old inmate of the cottage her little home might seem to be to me a veritable Naboth's vineyard.

'Ah! but I haven't done with it yet,' she said, with a quaintness that almost brought the tears to my eyes; 'we're some rare old stickers here.'

I hastened to assure her that there was nothing of the spirit of the covetous king in me; that I hoped she would live for many years to come, and that it was only the beauty of her cottage which had forced me to make the remark. We had a good laugh over it together; they have a rare sense of humour, some of these old village people, though the quality may be lacking in the younger ones amongst them. 'Ah, well, you can never tell,' she said; 'a while ago I was that shaky I thought to myself, "I shan't be 'ere long", now I feel quite myself again. Well, you can say that you have met a very funny old woman this afternoon,' she added, with a dry quaintness. And we parted, both laughing together as she opened the little garden gate for me. Dear old body, may she live for many more years to enjoy her sweet little home!

L.S.

COWSHED AND STY

Among the fruit trees graze a few calves or a stray sheep, for the flocks are folded on outlying arable lands, and the cows feed in the low pastures of the vale. The latter are driven down each morning, returning to the homestead at night to be milked by the master who puts on a long white linen coat called a cow-gown, to protect his clothes from defilement when busied in the yard among the livestock. The air of the milking shed is heavy with the fragrant breath of the cows, as

they stand in their stalls patiently waiting to be disburdened of their load, and turning gentle questioning eyes on the farmer who passes to and fro – a ghostly figure in the dim light. Since he took to milking he tells me that he has ceased to suffer from chilled or chapped hands, and he displays them with some pride, claiming that despite his other rough work they are as smooth as 'the missus's.'

When his grandchildren whom he goes nearer spoiling than does his wife, are staying at the farm, they are allowed to suck up the warm milk through a clean straw from the frothing pails, and upon occasion to try their skill at milking. It is not often they succeed in extracting more than a few drops, and the farmer laughs and strokes the cows, declaring that they know a strange hand, and that no one can get through the job as quickly as himself – not even the fogger who feeds them.

Adjoining the cowhouses are well-littered sties where fattening hogs, by which the great hams are supplied, lead a brief existence of sybaritic ease. They are seldom seen in public, preferring the luxurious seclusion of the inner sty, whence their small feet and inadequate legs can with difficulty support their unwieldy carcases the short journey to and from the feeding troughs.

A striking contrast to these serene mountains of flesh is the lean-flanked sow next door. Round her swarm her numerous progeny that now launch themselves with clamorous demands upon their resigned and blinking mother, now disperse over the sty, grunting, squealing, quarreling and poking their impudent

117

little black snouts into ever nook and cranny. Nature commits a fatal error in denying them the gift of perpetual youth. Hard fate, from a little pig to become a big one! Not only to lose day by day something of the infantine grace given at birth, but to develop ugliness and vice out of all proportion to that grace! To embody in short everything that is least desirable in character and appearance!

Eleanor Hayden

JUBILEE CELEBRATION DINNER AT HUNGERFORD

The arrangements for the dinner were of a most complete character, and reflected the greatest credit upon those who had the superintendence and upon the many willing helpers who rendered valuable assistance. The general control was chiefly with the secretary, who devoted much time and thought to the perfecting of the organization. So great, however, was the task that division of responsibility was imperative; accordingly various gentlemen undertook the entire charge of the several departments of preparation. Messrs Beard and Neate engaged the necessary labour and personally directed the construction of the tables, and the provision of the covers and everything connected therewith; Messrs Cundell and Kidd purchased the meat, inspecting it in both its live and dead condition, a task they have special qualifications for executing; Mr Church undertook the purchasing of the potatoes, the delivery to the various persons who had undertaken to cook them, and their collection and delivery to the headquarters of the commissariat

POLITICAL MEETING, UFFINGTON

at the place of dining; Messrs Hurd and Rosier bought the bread and delivered it to the various tables; Messrs Neate and Adnams, the official ale-tasters, were responsible for the supply and quality of the various drinks, which included beer, lemonade, soda water; Messrs Marsh and Hurd made the necessary arrangements for the hire of the crockery; while to Mr Marsh was assigned the duty of arranging for the distribution of the joints, ingredients for the puddings, &c., to the many persons who had undertaken the cooking, and subsequent collection of the same, and delivery at the dining ground, an arduous task involving a large amount of detail, for the carrying through of which those best competent to judge assert he developed a positive genius. It was found imperatively necessary, in order to make the requisite provision with any degree of accuracy, to take a census of the adults and children over and under 12 years of age who were likely to participate in the feast. This imposed a large amount of labour upon the Committee, but was satisfactorily accomplished, and it was upon the tabulated returns that the estimates were based. It was found that 40 tables, each 60 feet in length, would be required for seating the large number of diners, for the satisfying of whose appetites were provided 2,000lbs. of meat, 80 mutton pies, 1,800lbs of plum pudding, 70 gallons of bread, and a quantity of beer equal to a pint for each person, with liberal supplies of soda water and lemonade for abstainers. Even of so insignificant a thing as the mustard 16lbs, was provided. As to where

GREAT WESTALL

SHUTE END, WOKINGHAM

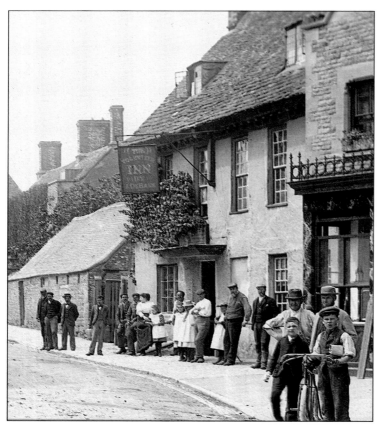

GLOUCESTER STREET, FARINGDON

the dinner should be held there was an even division of opinion amongst the members of the committee. One half were in favour of the streets as the place of meeting, and the other regarded the Mall as the more fitting. It was decided that it should be the latter by the casting vote of the Constable. The Mall and the adjoining Church Croft, which was also in part utilised for the occasion, certainly offered a most delightful meeting place. The agreeable shade from the prevailing sun which, after the long period of comparative sunlessness, has been so characteristic a feature of the Jubilee celebrations, the soft carpet of green turf, and the restfulness to the vision of the verdant landscape, formed a pleasant contrast to the exposure to the skies, the hardness and dustiness of the road, and the vista of bricks and mortar, which would have been accompaniments of a feast in the streets, while the ringing of the mellow sweet-toned bells of the parish church could scarcely fall as other than music even upon the irritated nerves of the correspondents who have been airing their bell-ringing grievances in the London papers. Dinner was timed for one o'clock, and was, considering the attendant circumstances, served with commendable promptitude shortly after that time. Each dinner ticket bore the number of the table at which its holder was to sit. In a central position, beneath a large awning, Messrs Beard and Phelps were busy receiving the various provisions and directing their distributions to the several tables. The cooking of the joints of meat, potatoes, and plum pudding,

THE WHEELER FAMILY, SULHAM

and the making of the latter also, was, as before intimated, undertaken by private families, a recipe being forwarded to each to secure uniformity. Messrs Adnams, Kidd, Platt, Rosier, and Wall lent horses and vehicles, which were of great service in the distribution and collection of the various provisions. The Constable also placed the vacant Tannery House at the disposal of the committee, and Miss Liddiard kindly undertook there the making and cooking of the meat pies. It is impossible for us to enumerate the names of those who aided in the cooking of the viands, but the opinion was general that it had been most admirably executed, and those ladies who, at much trouble and inconvenience to themselves, undertook this work, will at least have the satisfaction of knowing that to them belongs no small share of the credit attaching to the most successful production of Tuesday's dinner. A blast on the ancient horn was the signal for the saying of grace by the Vicar, which, however, by the majority had to be taken as said. It was specially arranged that this should not be done until all the tables were fully supplied, thus ensuring a simultaneous commencement at all parts. To each of the 40 tables was appointed four carvers, 160 in all.

The number of tickets issued was 2,500, but those who dined, calculated by the simple expedient of counting the plates, were nearer 3,000 than that number, there being no desire to exclude anyone, but simply to prevent an invasion of outsiders. So ample, however, was the accommodation provided that room could have been found for a hundred or two more, while of the good things that went to make up the dinner, there was 'enough and to spare.'

Newbury Weekly News, 20 June 1897

THE PATRIOTIC BERKSHIRE LABOURER

> Throo aall the waarld owld Gaarge would bwoast,
> Commend me to merry owld England mwoast;
> While vools gwoes praating vur and nigh
> We stwops at whum, my dog and I.

Guide to Berkshire (1881)

121

MARKET PLACE, ABINGDON

PANGBOURNE WEIR

Sources & Photographic Details

TEXT

The page numbers given below relate to this book and not the page numbers of the source books.

The sources of the texts are as follows: The Abingdonian (1890) pp. 47, 48, 101; James Cornish *Reminiscences of Country Life* pp. 11, 14, 34, 35, 38, 39, 99, 102; Peter Ditchfield *Country Folk: A Pleasant Company* pp. 13, 27, 81, 98; Eleanor Hayden *Travels Round My Village* pp. 12, 29, 35, 52, 65, 80, 85, 113, 116; Arthur L. Humphreys *The Berkshire Book of Song, Rhyme and Steeple Chime* pp. 51, 88, 112, 121; Thomas Hughes *Tom Brown's Schooldays* p. 9; L.S. *Untravelled Berkshire* pp. 23, 24, 25, 68, 72, 76, 86, 90, 93, 97, 104, 105, 110, 112, 115; Victor Mallet *Life with Queen Victoria: Maria Mallet's Letters from Court 1887–1901* p. 95; Mrs Oliphant *The Domestic Life of the Queen* p. 62; William Gordon Stables *The Gentleman Gipsy* pp. 42, 82; Jane Taylor *Memories of Old Berkshire* pp. 18, 29, 39, 67; Queen Victoria *Letters of Queen Victoria 1886–1901* p. 63; Alfred Williams *Round About Middle Thames* p. 36; *Villages of the White Horse* pp. 51, 75, 84, 89, 107.

Newspaper extracts: *Berkshire Chronicle* (1889) p. 112, (1892) p. 22; *Newbury Weekly News* (1897) p. 189; *Reading Observer* (1892) p. 21.

Manuscript sources: Alexander Elliot *Diaries* (Berkshire County Record Office) pp. 32, 68, 96; Emma Thoyts *Old Berkshire Schoolgames* (Local Studies Library, Reading) pp. 28, 89.

ILLUSTRATIONS

The following credits and information on photographs used in the book are given in ascending page order. Where a source is frequently credited it is referred to by its initials only (key at end of credits list).

Endpapers (front), Boulter's Lock, Maidenhead, *c.* 1890 (Taunt); COS; Endpapers (back), Jubilee Tea for the aged in Grenfell Park, Maidenhead, 1897; LMS. Page i, Buckland post office, *c.* 1915 (Taunt); COS. Page i, Hinton Waldrist post office, *c.* 1900 (Taunt); COS. Page iii, Faringdon market place, *c.* 1897 (Taunt); COS. Page iv, Oxford Rd/West St, Reading, *c.* 1900 (Dann); MERL. Page 1, A Reading cricket team, *c.* 1900 (Dann); MERL. Page 2, Cruck Cottage in Manor Road, Didcot, *c.* 1900; Brian Lingham. Page 3, The Castle Inn, Hurst, *c.* 1910; LMS. Page 4, The photograhic studio of Henry Beaufoy Wilder in the grounds of the old Rectory, Sulham. The Wilder family called it the 'Crystal Palace', 1890s (Wilder); Iris Moon. Page 5, Frances Dann photographed in old age in her own studio, *c.* 1895; MERL. Page 7, Burghfield post office, *c.* 1900; MERL. Page 8, Huntley and Palmer's biscuit tin labels, *c.* 1895; URA. Page 9, Berkshire Downs near West Ilsley, *c.* 1895 (Taunt); COS. Page 10, the schoolhouse and Mrs Smith at Hinton Waldrist, *c.* 1900 (Taunt); COS. Page 11, Chapel Lane, Uffington, *c.* 1900 (Taunt); COS. Page 12, The Smithy, Mill St, Wantage, *c.* 1900; VDM. Page 13, hand flailing (threshing), (Taunt); MERL. Page 14, Flour mill waggon at Bracknell, MERL. Page 15, Haymaking at Lockinge, *c.* 1906; MERL. Martha and Francis Dyer harvesting at Brimpton, *c.* 1895; MERL. Page 16, The George and Dragon at Swallowfield; MERL. Page 17, Cottage and family at Uffington, *c.* 1916. (Taunt); COS. Carter at Letcombe Regis, *c.* 1895; VDM. Page 18, Wantage

tramway engine no. 4, *c.* 1918; VDM. Page 19, Fox and Hounds at Waltham St Lawrence, *c.* 1900; MB. Page 20, Sulham Farm, *c.* 1895; Iris Moon. Page 21, Wokingham Workhouse, Board of Guardians meeting room, *c.* 1900 (Treacher); MERL. Page 22, Huntley and Palmers biscuit factory in Reading, *c.* 1880; URA. Page 23, Huntley and Palmers biscuit factory, Reading, *c.* 1899; URA. Page 24, Old Town Hall and Market Place Faringdon, *c.* 1901 (Taunt); COS. Page 25, Faringdon cattle market Church St, *c.* 1904 (Taunt); COS. Page 26, London St, Faringdon, *c.* 1904 (Taunt); COS. Page 27, White Horse Hill, *c.* 1900 (Taunt); VDM. Page 28, Down's Bottom Cottages at West Ilsley, *c.* 1900 (Taunt); COS. Page 29, Children playing under walnut trees at Bisham, *c.* 1885 (Taunt); COS. Page 30, The Green at Drayton, *c.* 1900 (Taunt); VDM. Lewis Stafford Northcote haymaking with his nanny in East Hendred, 1909; VDM. Page 31, Donnington Castle Farm, *c.* 1880; NDM. Page 32, Regatta on the Thames at Windsor, *c.* 1885 (Taunt); COS. Page 33, Windsor Castle from the Windsor river bank, *c.* 1893; WRCA. Page 34, The winners at Newbury Races, 1909; Peter Walwyn. Page 35, Seven Barrows, the house and tennis court, Lambourn, 1896; Peter Walwyn. Page 36, Boar's Head Inn, Friar St, Reading, *c.* 1900; MB. Page 37, The maltings at Simond's Brewery in Bridge St, Reading, *c.* 1905; Gordon Collier. Ock St Morris Men with the Ock St horns, 1909 (Hemmings Bros); AM. Page 38, The Bell Inn, South Westall; MERL. Amersham, *c.* 1890; MERL. Page 39, Haycart accident at Cookham, *c.* 1900 (Treacher); MERL. Page 40, The gatekeeper, Cookham Dean, *c.* 1905 (Treacher); MERL. Page 41, Twyford St in snow, *c.* 1900 (Treacher); MERL. Page 42, Hand-bell ringers at Newbury; MERL. Page 43, 'The Wanderer' caravan, commissioned and used by William Gordon Stables from the 1880s; Nostalgia Exhibitions. Page 44, Church Street, Twyford, *c.* 1908 (Treacher); MERL. Page 45, Thatcham Broadway celebrations for coronation in 1911; NDM. William Gordon Stables; Caravan Club. Page 46, Cookham, 1900 (Treacher); MERL. Page 47, Abingdon School Regatta, *c.* 1895 (two pictures); Abingdon School. Page 48; Abbey Bridge and mill, Abingdon, *c.* 1900; Abingdon School. Page 49, Crowds following a procession by Abingdon School which included boys on bicycles *c.* 1895; Abingdon School. Page 50, Wedding of Edward Coxeter and Miss Griswood at Abingdon, 1900 (Kerslake); VDM. Page 51, Coopers at Morland's Brewery, 1890s; Abingdon Museum. Page 52, Greengrocer's cart in Burghfield, *c.* 1900; MERL. Page 53, Farm labourer and his wife at Sulham, *c.* 1900 (Wilder); Iris Moon. Page 54, Ludbridge Mill at East Hendred, *c.* 1900; VDM. Page 55, Vachel Almshouses, corner of Castle St and Coley St, Reading, *c.* 1890; LMS. Page 56, The mill at Charney Bassett, *c.* 1900; RM. Page 57, Flower Show at Twyford, *c.* 1905 (Treacher); MERL. Page 58, Cottage at Upton; MERL. Page 58, Prize-winner at Twyford Flower Show, *c.* 1905 (Treacher); MERL. Page 59, Church at Shinfield (Collier); MERL. Page 60, Horn Street, Reading, 1880s; LMS. The Griffin Inn, Reading, 1890s; RM. Page 61, The 'Special Poultry Class' at the old University College in Valpy Street, Reading, 1897; URA. Page 62, Windsor Castle, Round Tower and Lower Ward, *c.* 1895; WRCA. Queen Victoria attending to her correspondence at Frogmore, Windsor, 1890s; RBC. Page 63, High Street, Windsor, *c.* 1893; WRCA. Page 64, Queen Victoria dining in the Oak Room at Windsor Castle with her daughter Beatrice, her daughter's husband, Prince Henry of Battenberg and their children Prince Alexander (back view), Princess Victoria Eugenie and Prince Leopold of Battenberg, 1895 (Steen); WRCA. Page 65, The Grandstand at Ascot, *c.* 1900 (Collier); MERL. Page 66, An unknown gathering for a service at Donnington Castle near Newbury, early 1900s; NDM. Page 67, The Royal Oak at Waltham St Lawrence, *c.* 1900; MB. Page 68, An unknown gathering at Theale, early

1900s; MERL. Page 69, Bray, *c.* 1885 (Taunt); COS. Uffington, *c.* 1916 (Taunt); COS. Page 70, Setting eel traps on the river Thames near Reading, 1880s; LMS. Page 71, A Berkshire water carrier and his cart; MERL. Page 72, Fishing in the Thames near Reading, 1880s; LMS. Page 73, The Blade Bone Inn, Bucklebury, *c.* 1900; MERL. Fishing in the Wilts and Berks Canal near Wantage in 1890s; VDM. Page 74, The Bridge at Newbury, *c.* 1900; RM. Page 75, Thames Lock, Cookham, *c.* 1880 (Taunt); COS. Page 76, Sheep Fair at East Ilsley, 1890s; RM. Page 77, Sheep Fair at East Ilsley 1906 (Taunt); COS. Page 78, Cemetery Road junction, Reading, early 1900s (Dann); MERL. Page 79, Shepherds on the Berkshire Downs; MERL. Page 80, Statue of King Alfred of Wantage market place, *c.* 1895 (Taunt); COS. Page 81, Cherry Pickers in Gordon Bosley's orchard, Harwell, *c.* 1900; VDM. Page 82, William Wing (second from left) and friends at the Roebuck Inn, Tilehurst, Reading, 1880s; LMS. Page 83, The George Hotel, Pangbourne, *c.* 1880 (Taunt); COS. Page 84, Pangbourne station, c. 1864 (Wilder); Iris Moon. Page 85, Streatley, the mill seen from the lane, *c.* 1880 (Taunt); COS. Page 86, The Willows, basket maker, Twyford, *c.* 1900; MERL. Page 87, Wallingford Bridge and toll-gate, *c.* 1870.; LMS. Page 88, Beenham, *c.* 1900; Sue Hopson. Page 89, Maypole dancing in Wright's Meadow, Uffington, *c.* 1916 (Taunt); COS. Page 90, Haymaking at Lockinge, *c.* 1906; MERL. Page 91, Cottage and old lady at West Ilsley, *c.* 1900 (Taunt); COS. Page 92, The Lion statue in Forbury Park, Reading, early 1900s (Dann); MERL. Page 93, Uffington Castle, bank holiday picnic, *c.* 1900 (Taunt); COS. Page 94, Schoolboy gardeners at Uffington, *c.* 1916 (Taunt); COS. Page 95, Windsor Bridge, *c.* 1888 (Taunt); COS. Princess Alice of Albany at Windsor Castle, 1886 (Cartland); RBC. Page 96, Six clergymen in a garden at Wantage, *c.* 1900 (Taunt); COS. Page 97, Lambourne railway station, *c.* 1890; MERL. Page 98, Life Guards outside the George Hotel, Lambourne, *c.* 1890; NDM, Page 99, Annual walking race from the Guild Hall Club, Bartholomew Street, Newbury, 1903; NDM. Studio photograph of unknown little girl, *c.* 1900; NDM. Page 100, Croquet on the lawn at Sulham House, *c.* 1900 (Wilder); Iris Moon. Rober Law and his grandaughter, Mary Ellen Parsons, *c.* 1900; NDM. Page 101, Daphne and Hary Mansell Plydell in the garden at Thorpe Lea House, near Windsor, 1880s; MERL. Page 102, Abingdon market place, church of St Nicholas and Abbey gateway, *c.* 1880 (Taunt); COS. Page 103, Silver Street, Reading, *c.* 1890 (Taunt); COS. The Old Angel Inn, Theale, *c.* 1910; MERL. Page 104, Staff of the Albert Laundry, Windsor, early 1900s; RBC. Page 105, Reading Natural History Society on an excursion to Bucklebury, 1881; LMS. Page 106, Francis Dyer and others making hoops for casks in a Berkshire wood, *c.* 1895; MERL. Page 107, The Greyhound, Besselsleigh, 1906 (Taunt); COS. Page 108, Biscuit packing room, at Huntley and Palmers' factory, Reading, 1899; URA. School of Art at Valpy Street, Reading, 1890s; URA.Page 109, Wargrave, *c.* 1890 (Taunt); COS. Morland's Brewery, Abingdon, *c.* 1890; MB. Page 110, Bridge Street, Sonning, *c.* 1900 (Taunt); COS. William Lailey, wooden bowl maker of Bucklebury, c. 1900; MERL. Page 111, The Bell, Shurlock Row, *c.* 1900; MB. Postman delivering an order of Sutton's Seeds from Reading, *c.* 1905; MERL. Page 112, The Hole in the Wall inn, Oxford Road, Pangbourne Reach, *c.* 1887 (Taunt); COS. Page 113, Wokingham market, *c.* 1895; Mr and Mrs K Goatley. Page 114, Families of the groom and coachman, Kingston Lisle, *c.* 1900 (Taunt); COS. Newbury Broadway, 1890s; NDM. Page 115, Newbury Borough Fire Brigade, Town Mills Yard, *c.* 1878; NDM. Reading, town hall and St Lawrence's church, *c.* 1900 (Dann); Twyford. Page 116, Elisha Hicks' Rose Nursery, Twyford; Twyford Local History Soc. Page 117, Steam lorry in Reading, *c.* 1900; LMS. Old Caversham Bridge, Reading, 1880s; LMS. Page 118, The fountain, St Mary Butts, Reading, 1887 (Taunt); COS. Mother and child photographed in a studio in Hungerford, *c.* 1910 (Parsons); Roger Pope. Page 119, Political meeting on the common at Uffington, *c.* 1900 (Taunt); COS. Outside The Crown at Great Westall, *c.* 1900; MERL. Page 120, Shute End, Wokingham, *c.* 1900; Mr and Mrs K Goatley. Gloucester Street, Faringdon, *c.* 1895 (Taunt); COS. Page 121, The Wheeler family at Sulham, *c.* 1900 (Wilder); Iris Moon. Page 122, Shopfront of Baylis and Co, Market Place, Abingdon (Taunt); COS. Pangbourne weir showing the rear of the Swan Inn, *c.* 1885 (Taunt); COS.

Key: AM Abingdon Museum. COS Centre for Oxfordshire Studies, Oxford. LMS Royal County of Berkshire, Library and Museum Service. MB Morland's Brewery, Abingdon. MERL Museum of English Rural Life, University of Reading. NDM Newbury and District Museum. RBC Royal Borough Collection, Windsor. RM Reading Museum. VDM Vale and Downland Museum, Wantage. WCRA Windsor Castle, Royal Archives © 1992 Her Majesty the Queen. URA University of Reading, Archives.